LEAD ANYWAY

TEACHING THROUGH THE FOG
WHEN THE SYSTEM STOPS
SEEING YOU

DR. KARISSA THOMAS

Lead Anyway: Teaching Through the Fog When the System Stops Seeing You

Copyright © 2025 by Dr. Karissa Thomas
All rights reserved.

No part of this publication may be reproduced, stored in a retrieval system, or transmitted in any form or by any means—electronic, mechanical, photocopying, recording, or otherwise—without the prior written permission of the publisher, except in the case of brief quotations embodied in critical articles or reviews.

For permissions or inquiries, contact:
Mosaic Intelligence Publishing

mosaicintelligencepublishing.com
contact@drkarissathomas.com

Printed in the United States of America

ISBN: 978-1-968277-01-7

Library of Congress Control Number: 2025909271

Interior Design: Marigold Emal

The content of this book is based on the author's professional experience, research, and personal insight. Any resemblance to actual persons, schools, or institutions is purely coincidental unless otherwise noted. The views expressed are those of the author and do not necessarily reflect those of any affiliated organization.

ACKNOWLEDGMENTS

To every educator who stayed when it was easier to leave—this book is for you.

To the leaders who prioritized presence over performance, courage over control—thank you.

To the students who taught me more than any textbook ever could—you're the reason I still believe.

Deep gratitude to the communities that shaped my story across the U.S., the Middle East, and beyond. Thank you to my family, my ancestors, and every mentor who invested in my journey when the path wasn't clear.

To those who held space for my healing while I supported others—your care made this book possible.

DEDICATION

To Christine Cobham
Head Teacher (College Director), The Oxford Partnership College of Excellence, Saudi Arabia – 2020

Your leadership was a masterclass in presence, principle, and quiet strength.
In a time of global uncertainty, you embodied steadiness.
In a system full of pressure, you modeled grace and dignity.

You led not just with vision, but with care.
And in doing so, you reminded us all what leadership can—and should—look like.

With sincere respect and enduring admiration.

CONTENTS

Foreword xi
By Henry Mutumba

Preface xv
Why This Book, Why Now

Introduction xvii
Teaching in the Trenches: The Unseen Emotional Cost of Leading Today

The Mosaic Intelligence Method™:
A Framework Overview xix
A Framework Overview

Part I: The New Reality of Schools 1
Chapter 1: The New Landscape of Learning 5
Disruption, Disengagement, and the Death of the Old Model

Chapter 2: Disconnection in a Connected Age 11
Tech Addiction, Digital Noise, and the Fight for Presence

Chapter 3: Teaching Through the Fog:
Emotional Leadership When Energy Is Low 19
Student Apathy, Emotional Shutdown, and the New Faces of Resistance

Chapter 4: Beyond the Label:
Seeing Students in Their Full Humanity 31
Identity, Inclusion, and the Classroom as a Mirror of Culture

Chapter 5: Teacher Burnout Is Not a Badge of Honor 41
Naming the Invisible Load and Reclaiming Emotional Wellness

Part II: Leading Beyond the Job Description 49

Chapter 6: When the System Doesn't See You 53
The Emotional Reality of Teaching Under Pressure

Chapter 7: Reimagining School Leadership 61
Principals, APs, and the Shift from Control to Connection

Mosaic Intelligence in Practice 69
Leading Beyond Titles

Chapter 8: Hard Conversations in Fragile Spaces 71
Navigating Pushback, Parent Tension, and Teacher Fatigue

Chapter 9: Restoring Culture Without Toxic Positivity 79
Building Trust, Accountability, and Belonging from the Ground Up

---

Part III: Courageous Classrooms, Brave Leaders 87

Chapter 10: Lead Anyway 91
Finding Purpose in the Mess and Meaning in the Work

Chapter 11: From Compliance to Courage 97
Creating Classrooms That Liberate, Not Just Instruct

Chapter 12: Centering Student Voice Without Losing Your Own 107
Boundaries, Listening, and the Art of Mutual Respect

Chapter 13: What the Data Doesn't Show 113
Measuring Growth in Ways That Matter

Chapter 14: Wholeness as a Leadership Strategy 125
You Can't Pour from an Empty Cup—But You Can Lead from a Full One

Chapter 15: Lead Anyway – The Invitation to Evolve 133
A Manifesto and Reflection Guide for Brave Educators in a Broken System

Lead Anyway Tools 140
Practical Moves for the Mosaic Classroom

Part IV: The Deep Work of Healing and Leading 147

Chapter 16: The Culture of Collective Care 149
How We Lead Together, Not Alone

**Chapter 17: When Leadership Fractures:
Reclaiming the Pieces** 157
Wholeness Is Not a Performance—It's a Return

Chapter 18: Lead Anyway—Now and Next 163
Sustaining Wholeness in Systems That Still Forget You

Interlude 169
Leading While Healing: When You've Been Harmed by the System

Higher Ed Interlude 173
*Lead Anyway in the Academy: Faculty,
Adjuncts, and the Hidden Curriculum of Survival*

Closing Reflections 179

Legacy Letter to Educators 181
A Closing Word from Dr. Karissa Thomas

Lead Anyway: Final Reflections and Courage Questions ... 183
*A Companion Section with Journal Prompts,
Scenarios, and Leadership Micro-Practices*

Appendices 191
- References 193
- Glossary 195
- About the Author 199

FOREWORD

It's an honour to contribute to Lead Anyway, a timely and deeply resonant work by Dr. Karissa Thomas. As an educator from Uganda who has taught in the United Kingdom and abroad, I've learned that our responsibility goes beyond delivering content—we also need to be emotional anchors in unpredictable systems.

When I met Dr. Karissa Thomas in Dubai, I recognized in her the kind of educator every system needs but few truly nurture. We were both teaching business, navigating cultural complexities, and leading classrooms that demanded more than just subject knowledge. They required presence, humanity, and vision.

Lead Anyway is more than a book—it's a vital intervention. It speaks directly to teachers, assistant principals, and leaders who quietly shoulder burdens within systems yet remain overlooked, undervalued, or unseen. Dr. Thomas writes with a depth born from lived experience. She provides not just strategies, but solidarity. Not just leadership jargon, but a lifeline.

As a school leader, I once supported a colleague through a conflict by helping her reconsider her approach to a misunderstanding with another teacher. Instead of intervening directly, I created space for her to reflect on the situation from different perspectives. Through active listening and asking guiding questions, I helped her shift from a reactive stance to a more empathetic and solution-oriented mindset. This change empowered her to begin a constructive conversation with the other teacher, resulting in better communication and collaboration.

That experience emphasized the importance of developing emotional intelligence, promoting peer-to-peer resolution, and practicing reflection—core aspects of my leadership approach.

As a British educator with Ugandan roots, I have spent my career navigating institutions that often overlook the richness we bring when leading from the margins. This book honours that richness. It challenges the idea that leadership must always be loud or traditional. Sometimes, leadership means choosing compassion when faced with silence. Sometimes, it involves creating belonging in spaces where none previously existed.

This academic year reminded me that leadership doesn't always come from the front of the room or a formal title—it can happen in a quiet planning session after school.

A colleague approached me, feeling overwhelmed by a particularly tough class. She was frustrated, exhausted, and unsure how to connect with her students. We met after school—just the two of us, a table, and a shared dedication to the students. Over an hour, we revised her lesson plan, emphasizing active strategies, student voice, and clear routines. I shared a few techniques that worked in my own classes, but mainly, I listened and helped her brainstorm what might work best for her group—focusing on creating possibilities rather than achieving perfection.

A week later, she told me the lesson went better than expected. "They actually participated," she said, smiling. "It felt like a win."

That small moment reminded me that leadership is often about service—quiet, supportive, and built on trust. It reaffirmed my belief: when teachers help each other, students succeed.

This book is a companion for anyone who understands what it means to care deeply and lead quietly. It doesn't offer empty motivation. Instead, it provides reflection, resonance, and authentic truth. Karissa has articulated what many of us feel but rarely say— that leadership in education requires as much emotional courage as it does policy or position.

To every reader holding this book: you are not invisible. You are essential. You are part of a global movement of educators who are redefining what it means to show up—with wisdom, resilience, and emotional integrity.

This is your permission to lead anyway.

As you read, may you feel seen, strengthened, and called to lead anyway.

- Henry Mutumba

PREFACE

Why This Book, Why Now

This book draws from my doctoral research on educator identity, emotional labor, and unseen leadership across both international and domestic settings.

I did not write this book because I had all the answers. I wrote it because I experienced the questions. The questions came up during moments of silence, resistance, burnout, and quiet breakthroughs—these are the kinds of questions that do not show up on evaluation rubrics but shape the very soul of this work.

I have led classrooms where students stopped showing up emotionally—long before they physically left. I have supported teachers who gave more than they had and then blamed themselves for breaking down. I have sat in meetings where we discussed the real issues indirectly because telling the truth would have been too costly. I have done these things both nationally and internationally, and I know that we all face the same school politics around the world. Behind every good instructor will always be the priority of the students—but behind every strong teacher, there must be emotional sustainability.

This need for emotional sustainability isn't just anecdotal—it's supported by research. My doctoral studies explored how teachers—particularly those in cross-cultural and international school settings—manage identity fragmentation, emotional dissonance, and the challenge of maintaining a sense of belonging in unfamiliar environments. What stood out was a consistent pattern: the emotional effort involved in teaching is both intense and often overlooked. Educators are constantly balancing their sense of self while taking on roles that rarely acknowledge the full extent of their humanity.

What I have observed in education—at every level—goes beyond burnout. It includes emotional exhaustion, cultural loss, identity fragmentation, and a deep desire to be seen not just as a professional but as a person. Many educators are not just exhausted; they are invisible, unheard, and unsupported in ways that words alone cannot fix.

This book is not a manual or a program. It isn't a collection of strategies to "fix" schools. Instead, it reflects what happens when educators choose to lead regardless — through the fog, amid fragmentation, in forgotten spaces. It serves as a call to return to ourselves so we can lead others with presence and purpose.

If you have ever felt invisible within a system that demands everything and gives little in return, this book is for you. If you have ever wondered whether it is possible to teach with courage while still protecting your own humanity, this book is for you. And if you have ever considered walking away because you could not keep dividing yourself in half to do the job, then this book is especially for you.

Now is the time for leadership that is emotionally honest, culturally responsive, and personally sustainable. Not later. Not when things calm down. Not when someone gives you permission. Now.

Because the fog isn't lifting, neither are we. Choosing to lead anyway — fully, imperfectly, and without losing our humanity — is the most revolutionary act we can take.

INTRODUCTION

Teaching in the Trenches: The Unseen Emotional Cost of Leading Today

You don't need to be in a crisis to feel like you're falling apart. For many teachers, stress doesn't strike all at once — it gradually builds up. It shows up as Sunday night dread, the silence after a lesson that didn't go well, quiet tears in the car, or the voice you use in meetings that no longer feels like your own.

I remember these moments in my own career, and I know many other educators do too. If it's not the students, it's the administrators. If it's not the administrators, it's the parents—or even your loved ones—complaining about how often you're grading papers and not prioritizing family time. The pressure comes from all sides, yet we keep showing up.

We don't often recognize the emotional toll of this work. We are asked to lead in systems that demand perfection while we're grieving, that require productivity while we're barely holding ourselves together, and that celebrate our strength while ignoring our strain. In today's educational landscape, we are expected to accomplish more with less—less time, less support, less empathy. We carry the trauma of students, the burden of policy failures, and the loneliness of always being the ones who "have it together." But we are not machines. We are not neutral. We are human.

This book isn't here to criticize the system just for criticism's sake. It aims to reveal the truth about the fog many of us are navigating—and to remind you that your leadership still matters. Behind every lesson plan is a person. Behind every data point is a tired decision. Behind every school that keeps moving forward is a team of people choosing, day after day, to care.

We don't just need more strategies; we need new permission—permission to feel, to question, to lead differently. If you're reading this and feeling tired but still searching for meaning and purpose, know this: you are not alone. You are part of a new kind of leadership quietly rising in classrooms, offices, and campuses around the world.

And this book? It's your companion on that journey. It also introduces the Mosaic Intelligence Method™—a leadership framework designed to help you lead with emotional integrity, cultural flexibility, and identity agility in an era when education demands more humanity than ever before. As we move forward together, you'll discover that leading anyway doesn't require perfection. It simply calls for presence, alignment, and a return to wholeness — not just for our students, but for ourselves.

Over eight years ago, I officially began studying what I had already experienced: the emotional strain of teaching in different cultural environments. My doctoral research explored how identity, belonging, and emotional resilience develop for Western educators working abroad. What I found—through interviews, observation, and reflection—was that the emotional challenges faced by educators are not only widespread but often go unnoticed. Lead Anyway continues that work. It's a message to every educator dealing with emotional dissonance, cultural hurdles, and the quiet exhaustion of always being the one who stays.

Let's begin.

THE MOSAIC INTELLIGENCE METHOD™: A FRAMEWORK OVERVIEW

Before we start, it's essential to understand the perspective this book takes. The Mosaic Intelligence Method™ is not a program, script, or checklist. It is a leadership framework built on the real experiences of educators who deal with emotional labor, identity fragmentation, and cultural complexity—often without recognition or support.

This approach emerged from my doctoral research on teacher identity and emotional labor in international and high-pressure education systems. What I found was a consistent need for a new kind of leadership—one that is emotionally grounded, culturally responsive, and identity-aware. The Mosaic Intelligence Method™ offers that solution.

It is built around three core capacities:

- **Emotional Integrity**
  The ability to lead honestly about your emotional state, to recognize the unseen effort you put in, and to foster psychological safety—for yourself and others. Emotional integrity isn't about having everything together. It's about showing up with presence, not performance.

- **Cultural Flexibility**
  The ability to adapt with humility, curiosity, and awareness in cross-cultural or diverse learning settings. It involves releasing rigid assumptions, listening more than lecturing,

and leading in ways that honor—not erase—the lived experiences of others.

- **Identity Agility**
  The ability to stay true to who you are while adaptively responding to the changing identities around you. This involves managing systemic roles, societal expectations, and internal questions about belonging—without losing your sense of self.

These three capacities are interconnected. They form a leadership approach that prioritizes presence over pressure, belonging over compliance, and wholeness over burnout. You will see them demonstrated, questioned, and examined in each chapter that follows — not as ideals, but as calls to lead with more humanity.

As you read this book, I encourage you to keep these three capacities in mind. Notice where they show up in your work. Observe where they are missing in your school culture. And most importantly, notice how things change when you start leading with them.

The Mosaic Intelligence Method™ is not the endpoint. It serves as the compass, guiding us toward what leadership can be when we stop merely performing and begin truly becoming.

You Are Not an Afterthought: The Educator's Evolution Matters

In education, it's easy to focus entirely on students—and while they deserve our utmost care, so do you.

Your identity as an educator is not fixed. It constantly evolves—shaped by personal history, institutional demands, cultural expectations, and emotional resilience. This book isn't just about pedagogy; it's about you. Who you are becoming. What you're carrying. And how your personal growth is as important as any curriculum you teach.

The research supports this idea. A 2021 study published in *Teaching and Teacher Education* found that teachers who engaged in reflective identity development experienced significantly greater resilience, job satisfaction, and ability to connect with students. My own doctoral research confirmed this: educators who actively explored their evolving identity—especially in cultural or high-stress settings—were more likely to maintain long-term emotional health and find a sense of purpose even in environments prone to burnout.

In other words: your wholeness matters. Not just for you, but for your students. When you grow, they benefit. When you reclaim yourself, they see what self-reclamation looks like. When you protect your emotional integrity, they are more likely to protect theirs.

This book emphasizes your evolution—not as an afterthought, but as a central element in sustainable, liberating, and emotionally intelligent leadership.

Who We Teach: The Reality of Today's Students

Our students are not the same as they used to be—and this is not a criticism. It's a call for clarity.

Today's learners are experiencing mental health challenges at record highs. According to the CDC's 2023 Youth Risk Behavior Survey, over 40 percent of high school students reported feeling persistently sad or hopeless. Rates of anxiety, depression, and trauma-related symptoms have risen sharply across K–12 and higher education. The American College Health Association states that nearly 75 percent of college students faced moderate to severe psychological distress in the past year.

But emotional health is just one layer. Students today are also:

- Exploring fluid identities related to gender, race, culture, and neurodiversity.
- Navigating economic instability, climate grief, and political disillusionment.
- Surrounded by constant digital noise, algorithmic influence, and social comparison.
- Holding family roles—such as caregiving, translating, and surviving—that influence their learning presence.

- Questioning power structures, traditional authority, and the true relevance of education.

In short, they are emotionally intense, identity-driven, and culturally intricate.

This is important. Because if we treat these students as if they are the same as they were ten years ago—or even five—we will completely miss them. We will mistake apathy for defiance. We will view resistance as a problem. And we will unintentionally deepen the disconnection we're trying to fix.

The Mosaic Intelligence Method™ helps us connect with others where they are. Not through control, but through clarity. Not through fear, but through flexibility. Not with a script, but with emotional presence to lead through complexity instead of around it.

As we progress through this book, you'll observe examples of who these students are becoming—and who we, as educators, are also becoming in response. The aim is not to fix them or ourselves. The aim is to lead anyway—with honesty, presence, and the freedom to evolve.

PART I

The New Reality of Schools

DR. KARISSA THOMAS

When the Bell Rings, the Battle Begins

There's still a sound that marks the rhythm of a school day: the bell. But what once signaled the start of learning now signals something much more complicated. When it rings, teachers brace themselves—not just for teaching, but for interruptions, disconnections, tension, and fatigue. In today's schools, the job description never shows the whole picture.

Education has always required resilience, but what it demands now is something deeper—emotional depth, cultural fluency, and a clear sense of identity. The challenges educators face today are not just academic—they are human. A student's silence might indicate depression. An outburst could be a sign of trauma. A phone in hand is often not rebellion but a source of comfort. And behind every "unmotivated" child is a story no data sheet can capture.

We live in a world of constant change. Students walk into classrooms carrying grief, social anxiety, racial trauma, questions about identity, and digital dependence. Still, many educators are asked to teach as if nothing has shifted. To standardize learning in an unpredictable world. To discipline behavior when what's really needed is belonging. To hit performance goals while they are quietly burning out.

This is the truth we must face: the system still functions as if it's 2005, while the classroom reflects 2025. The gap between these two realities is where real leadership is needed.

Through my doctoral research on Western educators in international school settings, I discovered that emotional labor, identity fragmentation, and cultural displacement are not isolated experiences—they are common to modern teaching. Educators worldwide are stretched between who they are and the roles they are expected to fulfill. This book builds on that research, broadening the conversation to include every educator navigating the complexities at the intersection of self and system.

In this section, we identify what others avoid. We bring language to what teachers feel but rarely say out loud. These next few chapters are not about best practices; they are about honest truths. What's breaking down. What's burning out. And what we must reimagine if we want education to heal, grow, and matter again.

And this reimagining starts by adopting a new form of leadership—one that values humanity over hierarchy, presence over performance, and purpose over protocol. This is where the Mosaic Intelligence Method™ begins to come into focus: a framework that encourages us not just to do the work, but to become the kind of leaders our schools need now. Leaders who bring emotional integrity into staff rooms, cultural flexibility into classrooms, and identity agility into every decision they make.

The bell may still ring, but what happens after that? That's where you come in.

This marks the start of a new kind of leadership.

This is where you choose to lead regardless.

CHAPTER 1

The New Landscape of Learning

When the Old Rules Stopped Working

There was a time when structure alone could hold a classroom together. The bell rang, students sat down, and teachers taught. Routine, authority, and compliance were enough to carry a school year through. But that's no longer the case.

Today's classrooms—and lecture halls, Zoom rooms, and office hours—are a clash of complexity. Generational trauma, digital distractions, identity

"Education isn't failing—it's evolving. And it's asking us to evolve with it."

shifts, and systemic fatigue all compete for attention in a space once ruled by simple rules. The educational landscape has changed, yet many leaders keep teaching and managing as if it hasn't.

You don't need to be inside a K–12 school to feel it. College professors report alarming levels of disengagement and rising absenteeism. Adjunct faculty work with students who have full-time jobs, care for families, and silently struggle with mental health issues. The problem is widespread. From preschool to postgraduate studies, the education field is quietly falling apart under the pressure of expectations that no longer match reality.

DR. KARISSA THOMAS

The Emotional Labor of Teaching Today

Educators are not just delivering instruction—they are offering emotional support to learners in crisis. Whether you're managing a first-grade classroom or mentoring doctoral students, the role now includes responsibilities for which no syllabus or training prepared us: therapist, tech support, crisis manager, motivational coach, and sometimes, the only stable adult in a young person's life.

We are dealing with TikTok-inspired self-diagnoses, social media spirals, and a deep disengagement that looks like apathy but is often exhaustion in disguise. While students face anxiety, identity stress, or economic uncertainty, educators are still measured by outdated standards and mandates made for a different time. This isn't just student disengagement; it's a slow decay of institutions.

Hidden within that decay is the unspoken grief of educators who no longer believe they are making a difference. Yet, each year, new teachers enter classrooms with fresh energy and a vision for what learning can be. That spark matters—it can challenge systems that feel unbreakable. In today's connected world, a single teacher's influence can ripple far beyond what they will ever see. Former students can reach out or observe from afar through social media, sharing life updates, seeking advice, or simply letting you witness their journeys. It's a strange, beautiful, and sometimes bittersweet reality: teachers are no longer forgotten figures in a student's past but visible partners in their ongoing growth.

What My Research Revealed About Teacher Identity

Years before I wrote this book, I formally studied what I had already experienced in the field—the invisible identity shifts teachers endure when navigating cross-cultural complexity, emotional dissonance, and systems that rarely reflect their full humanity. My doctoral research explored Western educators working abroad and found that many were silently unraveling under the weight of emotional labor, fragmented identity, and the loss of cultural belonging. They weren't just teaching—they were constantly code-switching, adapting, absorbing, and suppressing. Their leadership was often relational, emotionally attuned, and deeply intuitive—but undervalued in systems that prioritized output over presence.

What I found in those stories reflects what educators are now facing worldwide. Whether in Abu Dhabi or Atlanta, the emotional burden is real. The fragmentation is real. And so is the call for a more grounded, human-centered leadership style that doesn't require us to leave parts of ourselves outside the classroom.

Outdated Tools in a New Terrain

Many school leaders and higher education administrators still try to motivate their staff and faculty with tools that no longer work—compliance charts, mandatory professional development, student evaluations, and public praise without private support. However, none of these address the real issue: we are emotionally underprepared for the world we're being asked to educate in.

Following a global pandemic, a digital takeover, and a worldwide identity crisis, a simple truth has become clear: old frameworks no longer work in new terrain. What used to be predictable is now uncertain. What was once a classroom has become a contested space for attention, authenticity, and connection.

We cannot discipline our way out of this. We cannot data-track our way back to meaning. We cannot mandate connection and expect creativity, healing, and resilience to come uninvited.

Instead, we need a new leadership perspective—one that sees clearly, feels deeply, and leads bravely. In the Mosaic Intelligence Method™, we recognize that we are always in motion—shaped by our culture, our identity, and our emotions. Every moment, even the hard ones, can be used as a building block toward something better, or left to spiral into the unknown. The choice is ours, and the compass we use matters.

This is the core of the Mosaic Intelligence Method™—not a checklist, but a compass. Born from real-world experience—not theory—it's designed to meet educators in the mess, not just the mission, guiding them with emotional integrity, cultural flexibility, and identity agility in classrooms and institutions that are anything but simple.

DR. KARISSA THOMAS

The Real Question Is: What Are We Rebuilding?

The question is no longer, "How do we get students back on track?" The real question is, "How do we co-create a new track altogether?"

Because what's breaking down is not just behavior or motivation—it's the infrastructure of education itself: the policies, priorities, and cultural contracts that once held the system together. These aren't problems a single classroom can fix. They are deep structural shifts that demand a response at every level—from local communities to national policy.

We cannot expect educators to carry society's burdens without tending to their emotional well-being. We cannot ignore identity, inequity, and innovation and still expect engagement to flourish. We cannot keep patching cracks in a wall when the foundation itself needs redesigning.

The truth? Education is not failing; it's evolving. And it's asking us to evolve with it—to lead with presence, not pressure. To see students not as problems but as mirrors. To see teachers and faculty not as tools but as people doing deeply human work in systems that weren't built for today's needs.

This is not a call to throw everything away. It is a call to honestly evaluate what no longer works and to lead forward—with wisdom, courage, and a willingness to redefine what learning can be in this new era.

Lead Anyway Reflection

- Where are you still trying to use outdated tools for modern problems?
- Which aspects of your leadership or instruction seem reactive rather than responsive?
- What have you silently grieved regarding your role in education—and how might you start to heal moving forward?
- In what ways have your students changed? Have you adapted how you see them?

> **TOOL TO TRY:**
> **Respond to Emotions First**

When student behavior changes, pause before redirecting. Ask yourself: "What might this student be feeling that I'm not noticing?" This self-check helps you shift from reacting to responding with insight.

> **TOOL TO TRY:**
> **Respond to Emotion Before Intervention**

Before diving into academic help or corrective feedback, address the emotion that's present. Even a brief acknowledgment ("I can see this is frustrating") can lower resistance and open the door for learning. Once the emotional temperature drops, then guide the student toward the skill or solution.

CHAPTER 2

Disconnection in a Connected Age

The Silence Behind the Screens

Ms. Allen stared at the sea of faces in her 9th-grade classroom. Every student was present—technically—but none were paying attention. Heads down. Earbuds in. Phones hidden but active under desks. She paused mid-sentence and asked, "What do you think about that last point?" A few looked up, confused. No one responded. The silence said it all.

> *"You can't out-teach emotional absence. But you can model presence that reconnects."*

Three floors up in a college building, Dr. Ramirez faced something eerily similar. A class discussion on racial identity that once energized the room now fell silent. Cameras were off. Mics stayed muted. No one responded. A comment box with a single "thanks" became the only sign of life. These weren't lazy students. They were simply… gone.

What we're witnessing goes beyond simple digital distraction; it shows emotional and relational disconnection openly.

DR. KARISSA THOMAS

When Tech Replaces Touch

Technology has transformed access to knowledge. However, it has also fragmented the human aspect of education. Students now feel more connected to their devices than to the people around them. Social media algorithms provide instant validation, while games deliver dopamine on demand. TikTok never runs out of entertainment. In contrast, genuine human interaction—especially when it involves vulnerability or sustained attention—feels heavier than ever.

We used to worry about students having too little access to the world. Now, we worry that they've absorbed so much of the world's chaos that they've become emotionally numb to it. Hyperconnectivity has become the norm, but it hasn't nurtured students in the way connection is meant to. They scroll constantly but rarely feel seen. They consume content relentlessly but express themselves selectively. They know how to "appear" present without truly being available.

Educators at all levels are noticing that students are not only distracted; they are also anxious, overstimulated, and emotionally distant in ways that feel unfamiliar—and sometimes, unfixable.

In my own fieldwork, I observed how identity conflict and emotional dissonance often go unspoken in professional settings, yet influence every interaction in the classroom. A teacher's unacknowledged fatigue, a student's unspoken grief—these are silent factors that shape engagement. We're not just teaching content; we're navigating human complexity within institutional constraints.

The Disengaged Student Is Not the Enemy

It's tempting to label disengaged students as disinterested, lazy, or disrespectful. But that's a misunderstanding. Often, what appears as apathy is actually a form of protection. A disengaged student isn't a problem to fix; they're a sign to pay closer attention.

In elementary classrooms, quiet students might not be inattentive. They could be overwhelmed by what they saw at home the night before. In middle schools, a student who won't look up might be struggling with social anxiety that takes precedence over the urgency of the lesson. In college lecture halls, a student who is absent might not be unmotivated; they could be working two jobs and hiding their panic attacks behind absences and excuses.

Disconnection isn't always a choice. Sometimes it's something we inherit, sometimes it's learned out of necessity, and other times it's the only way a student feels safe. Recognizing this isn't about lowering expectations—it's about humanizing the classroom.

The Educator's Dilemma: Compete or Connect

Educators are tired of competing with screens. And here's the hardest truth: we can't. No lesson plan, discussion prompt, or rubric will ever be as instantly satisfying as the algorithmic brilliance behind YouTube, TikTok, or Instagram. But that doesn't mean we're powerless. There's one thing technology cannot imitate: human presence.

Presence doesn't refresh or vanish, nor does it require perfection. It simply appears and remains. In every classroom, office, and Zoom window, presence fosters trust—not perfection or performance. When students feel emotionally seen — not just behaviorally managed — they start to re-engage with their own learning experience.

In this landscape, connection — not control — has become the most valuable currency in education. Educators who choose to lead relationally rather than reactively are redefining what real impact looks like. And this is why the Mosaic Intelligence Method™ does not start with external strategies or prescriptive solutions — it starts with self-awareness. With emotional integrity. With seeing yourself and your students as whole people navigating invisible pressures every day.

This reflects a key aspect of the Mosaic Intelligence Method™: emotional integrity combined with cultural flexibility in real time. It is leadership that comes from presence, not pressure. It is about reconnecting, human to human, in a world that constantly tries to pull us apart.

What the Research Says

A 2023 study published in the *Journal of Educational Psychology* confirmed what many educators have long suspected: student engagement is driven more by connection than by content. The research showed that students who felt recognized by at least one adult at their school were much more likely to stay motivated—even when facing mental health issues or external instability. In higher education, the results reflected similar patterns—perceived instructor presence in virtual and hybrid environments was a strong predictor of student persistence, satisfaction, and success.

These data points reflect findings from my own doctoral research, which examined identity, belonging, and emotional resilience among Western educators teaching abroad. In interviews with teachers in international school settings, a consistent theme emerged: when educators felt fragmented, emotionally unsupported, or unseen within the institutional structure, their capacity to maintain genuine connections with students declined. The disconnection wasn't just affecting students—it was affecting teachers as well. And without emotionally attuned leadership, that fragmentation only worsens.

These findings are expected. They confirm what many educators already do instinctively when they pause to ask a question, remember a student's name, or show grace during a deadline. It's not just about what we teach; it's about how we show up—and who we choose to be when the learning process feels vulnerable, frustrating, or uncertain.

A New Kind of Attention

In this age of digital overload, we need a new way to understand engagement. It can no longer be about perfect participation or complete silence. True engagement might look like a hesitant student making eye contact for the first time. It might sound like a question whispered after class instead of spoken aloud. It might develop slowly, quietly, and unpredictably. And that's okay.

We need to learn to lead with attention that is welcoming, not invasive; with curiosity rather than dominance; and with awareness that students are not blank slates but complete individuals navigating complex, layered emotional lives in a world that is louder and more intricate than ever before.

Disconnection may be common, but reconnecting is a daily priority. This process starts with us.

Sometimes it looks like pausing your lesson to notice when a student's shoulders finally relax. Other times, it's remembering to follow up on a quiet comment a student made and letting them know it mattered. It might be offering space without pressure, or a smile without demanding anything. These moments are not small—they are the new currency of trust in learning spaces.

What It Looks Like in Real Life

In a middle school hallway in Chicago, a teacher kneels to tie a student's untied sneaker—not because the student couldn't do it, but because they seemed too overwhelmed to try. That simple gesture earns a smile and, later that day, a completed assignment that had been missing for weeks.

In a rural community college, an adjunct professor logs into her virtual class five minutes early—not to prep slides but to greet students as they enter. One student, attending from a hospital waiting room, says quietly, "Thanks for still letting me come." The professor responds, "You being here matters. I see you." That exchange alone keeps the student enrolled.

In a fifth-grade classroom in California, a student who hasn't spoken all week suddenly raises their hand—not to answer but to ask for help. The teacher pauses the lesson and walks over, making eye contact and offering a calm presence without fanfare. Later, the student stays behind and says, "I just needed to know you wouldn't be mad."

This is the pedagogy of presence. It doesn't always show up in test scores or participation logs, but it appears in the climate of trust that develops over time. These moments don't need extra training—they call for intentional attention. They are micro-interventions, driven not by curriculum, but by connection.

When students feel acknowledged, they are more likely to stay. Not just in the classroom, but throughout the learning process itself. These moments of quiet connection may seem minor, but they plant the seeds of a new kind of leadership—one rooted not in authority, but in attunement. When we lead with genuine presence, we lead from within. We create environments where students do not have to earn belonging. By doing so, we become leaders whose influence endures beyond the lesson plan.

Presence is not just about how we teach; it's also about how we lead.

From Compliance to Commitment

Yes—some students will arrive unprepared. They might skip practice, avoid reading assignments, or treat class time as social hour. The temptation is to see these behaviors as proof they don't care. But disengagement is rarely just about willpower—it's about where attention feels safest to land. If we address that resistance only with correction, we may secure compliance but risk losing connection.

The alternative is to create conditions where effort feels less risky than avoidance. In a dance school, that might mean weaving social energy into warm-ups so that practice and play coexist. In a science lab, it might mean letting students design part of the experiment so their curiosity fuels the work. In any setting, it means showing students that preparation is not just expected — it's worth their time because someone is waiting to notice their growth.

When we change our perspective *from Why aren't they trying?* to *What makes trying feel possible here?*, we stop competing with their distractions and start encouraging their investment. The Mosaic Intelligence Method™ describes this as leading with emotional integrity and cultural agility in real time—meeting students where they are without leaving them there. It's not about lowering the standards; it's about building a bridge high enough for them to cross.

When we prioritize presence over pressure, we cease managing students and begin guiding them—from showing up out of obligation to showing up out of genuine interest.

Lead Anyway Reflection

- When was the last time your students or colleagues were physically present but emotionally absent? How did you respond at that moment?
- In what ways are you currently trying to compete with digital engagement rather than fostering human connection?
- What assumptions have you made about disengaged students that need re-evaluation?
- How do you demonstrate presence in your teaching or leadership—even when you're feeling tired?
- What simple ritual, phrase, or routine could you introduce to make your classroom or campus office feel like a space where students are truly welcomed and encouraged to be their full selves?

TOOL TO TRY:
The Emotional Weather Report

Start the class by asking, "What's the weather like inside today—sunny, cloudy, stormy?" Use the responses to gauge the emotional climate. This shifts your focus from performance metrics to human readiness, allowing you to teach based on the room you actually have.

TOOL TO TRY:
The One-Minute Anchor

Begin with a sixty-second pause—no agenda, no screens. Let students settle, breathe, and simply be present. This models that the work of learning starts with being here, not being perfect.

CHAPTER 3

Teaching Through the Fog: Emotional Leadership When Energy Is Low

The Classroom That Changed Nothing

Mr. Givens had prepared for this unit all summer. It was bold, relevant, and grounded in student voice. On day one, he arrived energized and armed with multimedia, case studies, and a clear learning arc. But by week two, something didn't resonate. Students weren't hostile or disruptive; they were just... flat. One student doodled in silence, another yawned into his hoodie, and a third asked to go to the bathroom but never returned.

"When clarity is impossible, compassion becomes your curriculum."

By week three, the silence started to sting. It wasn't indifference—it was something harder to name. Not resistance, but resignation. Mr. Givens stood at the front of the classroom and thought, "Am I the only one awake in here?"

He wasn't alone. Across the country and around the world, educators report the same unsettling feeling: they're teaching through fog. Not just intellectual confusion, but emotional heaviness. A kind of cognitive shutdown that doesn't show up on behavior charts or diagnostic manuals, but instead in the slow dimming of curiosity and will. It's as if students—and teachers—are running on fumes.

Yes, classrooms are full of energy. There are students who arrive curious, self-motivated, and deeply engaged. This book acknowledges their presence—in fact, we celebrate them. But that's not the focus here. This chapter isn't about the exceptions; it's about the new emotional baseline many educators are experiencing. A fog settles into rooms even when the curriculum is strong, the teacher is skilled, and intentions are pure. We mention this not to overlook the bright spots, but to highlight the emotional burden educators carry when the spark fades—and no one can quite explain why.

The Exhaustion We Don't Talk About

The fog isn't just in their minds. It's in the culture. It's in our staff meetings, our inboxes, and our living rooms. Educators are emotionally exhausted—and not just from workload. They're carrying grief, loss, anxiety, and a constant feeling of falling short. The invisible emotional labor of teaching has increased, but few have taken time to acknowledge it.

In my doctoral research on teacher identity and emotional labor in international schools, I noticed a clear pattern: teachers often struggle with fractured identities, torn between who they're expected to be and who they truly are. Many feel pressured to keep emotional stability even as they privately break down. This inner conflict drains not only their energy but also their authenticity—and ultimately, their impact.

We've normalized feeling overwhelmed. We praise resilience but ignore the cost. We send out more strategies, more PD links, and more newsletters. But what many educators actually need isn't another tool. It's permission to feel what the job asks of them—and space to breathe through it.

Students feel it too. They're navigating family instability, identity shifts, climate anxiety, algorithmic pressure, and cultural fragmentation. Many wake up already exhausted. School becomes just another environment demanding more from them than they can give. And so, they shut down—not to defy us, but to survive.

So, what is the response when the room falls silent—not with engagement, but with emotional exhaustion? Not a louder voice. Not another strategy. The invitation is presence. Leadership that listens before it acts. That perceives beyond immediate behavior. That allows both teachers and students to be human again. Sometimes, the most transformative move isn't to push through the fog—but to pause, acknowledge it, and choose to lead with care regardless.

Teaching When You're Not Okay

There's a quiet panic teachers feel when their best efforts meet blank stares, when the lesson that once sparked discussion now falls flat, and when even the most engaged students seem to fade away. In those moments, it's easy to spiral, question your effectiveness, and wonder if your work still matters.

But this is exactly when emotional leadership is most essential—not superficial positivity, but sincere honesty; not fake energy, but genuine presence.

There is strength in saying, "I feel it too," by naming the fog rather than pretending it's not there. Students don't need perfect teachers; they need real ones—those willing to be fully human in the room, even while maintaining structure and standards.

This is the moment when the **Mosaic Intelligence Method**™ springs into action—when emotional integrity takes precedence over strategy. When presence becomes pedagogy.

Emotional integrity encourages teachers to acknowledge their own feelings without shame, leading with honesty instead of repression. It takes the courage to say, "Today is hard," while still caring and setting boundaries. By doing so, educators show what it means to stay present, even when circumstances aren't perfect.

Cultural flexibility involves understanding that your classroom exists within larger societal currents—such as grief, social pressure, and instability—and that students may carry burdens that prevent traditional engagement. It means adjusting not by lowering expectations, but by changing how connections are made, how safety is ensured, and how voice is honored.

Identity agility challenges the idea that you must always lead from the same version of yourself. It allows you to evolve and to lead from different emotional states depending on what's real and needed. This is what enables a teacher to say, "I am still a strong educator, even on the days I feel fragile."

When you're not okay, you don't have to put on a show. You should teach from a place of depth, awareness, and grace. The Mosaic Intelligence Method™ doesn't shy away from tough moments — it acknowledges them. It reminds us that the wholeness of the teacher is just as important as the learning outcomes. And on foggy days, being human first is the most powerful way to teach.

The Myth of Constant Motivation

We've been told a myth that great teaching is always lively, inspiring, and energizing. But great teaching today often means showing up when no one claps, holding space when no one talks, planning thoughtfully even when energy is low, and leading with love when results are slow.

We can't depend on external validation to maintain internal conviction, especially now. The work of this era is very unglamorous; it's emotional trench work. The victories—when they happen—are often subtle: a flicker of engagement, a returned assignment, a question asked after class.

That doesn't lessen the significance of the work. In fact, it makes it sacred.

What the Research Says

Recent data from the RAND Corporation and the American Psychological Association show that educator burnout is at historic highs. Teacher morale has dropped sharply since 2020, with emotional exhaustion and secondary trauma as the primary factors. My own research further found that teachers experiencing identity fragmentation—especially in cross-cultural or high-pressure settings—reported feeling less that they belonged and withdrew emotionally more.

Student outcomes reflect these dynamics. Emotional dysregulation, increased absenteeism, and disengagement are not just student issues; they serve as systemic signals. But here's what the data also confirms: students are more likely to re-engage in environments where emotional safety is demonstrated—not dictated.

Emotional safety isn't created through compliance; it's fostered through connection. Classrooms that include relational routines, honest communication, and psychological space see higher levels of retention and trust. This is true from elementary to higher education, especially in international, multilingual, or hybrid learning settings where students also navigate cultural complexity.

The research clearly shows: emotional attunement isn't extra—it's vital. Identity-aligned leadership isn't optional—it's urgent.

Fog on the College Campus

Tara, an English professor at a community college, noticed her students were arriving later each week—some missing class entirely. But it wasn't because they didn't care. Many were juggling overnight shifts, parenting, and the emotional burden of being first-generation college students. Instead of tightening attendance policies, Tara started each class with a check-in question on the board: "What's one thing you need to leave outside this room today?" It became a quiet ritual that helped students breathe before they started—and reminded her that clarity in the fog often begins with compassion, not strict rules.

Leading Through, Not Around, the Fog

We don't need to wait for the fog to lift before we teach. However, we must adjust our teaching during it. That involves slowing down, asking authentic questions, allowing silence to linger, and integrating wellness into pedagogy—not as an add-on, but as a central element of lesson planning. It's about demonstrating how to be okay with not always feeling okay.

Teaching through the fog isn't ignoring it—it's moving through it anyway. With presence. With patience. With leadership that says: "I see you, even now."

This is not survival mode. Survival mode is reactive, operating on fumes, enduring the day, ignoring warning signs with gritted teeth and forced smiles. It's the burnout cycle disguised as resilience. But what we're discussing here is something entirely different.

Teaching through the fog with the **Mosaic Intelligence Method**™ isn't about pushing through—it's about leading in a new way.

It's a move from focusing on performance to emphasizing presence.

It's not about holding everything perfectly together. It's about holding space genuinely.

It's leadership that recognizes the complexity of the moment, resists defaulting to autopilot, and doesn't hide behind a scripted lesson when the energy in the room calls for something deeper.

Emotional integrity is what anchors you in this kind of leadership. It's what allows you to say, "I'm navigating this too," without collapsing under it. It's the practice of checking in with yourself—not after the day ends, but in real time, with enough self-awareness to model emotional literacy and relational steadiness for your students.

Cultural flexibility helps you see that the fog doesn't lift equally for everyone. Some students are dealing with layers of generational trauma, systemic instability, or cultural silence that influence how they show up—or don't. It's not about overcompensating or rescuing, but about changing how we interpret behavior, engagement, and silence. It's about leading with context, not assumptions.

Identity agility allows you to lead with subtlety. It enables you to fluidly switch between roles of teacher, mentor, learner, and human. It helps you adjust your leadership voice without losing authority. Some days, you might lead with clear direction; other days, through reflective dialogue. Identity agility confirms that both approaches are valid and that you don't need to stick to one version of yourself to be effective.

What It Looks Like in Real Life

Step into almost any classroom today, and the emotional atmosphere is clear. A high school student sits blankly at the board, earbuds hidden under their hoodie—not out of defiance, but from exhaustion. A middle school teacher repeats the same request four times in one period, only to find the student crying in their car during lunch. An elementary student who once colored inside the lines now flips desks or hides beneath them. These are not isolated incidents. They reflect a broader emotional climate.

The emotional dysregulation identified by the research doesn't come with a warning—it shows up as chronic lateness, refusal to finish tasks, or bursts of frustration that seem too strong for the situation. Beneath these behaviors are students trying to handle an emotional world that has become heavier, faster, and more complicated.

And teachers? They feel it physically: in the knots in their shoulders, in the decision fatigue by second period, and in the quiet resignation when a lesson they stayed up late to plan falls flat because half the class was absent—or emotionally unavailable.

Yet, even in this landscape, we glimpse what works.

A teacher who starts class with a one-minute breathing exercise—not because it's trendy, but because it sets the tone. A professor who pauses a lecture to ask, "How's your energy today?" and sincerely waits for the answer. A principal who allows staff to say, "I'm overwhelmed," without fear of being judged weak. These are small actions. But they have a ripple effect. They reshape the emotional climate. They remind students and teachers alike that we are still human here.

Emotional attunement is more than just a soft skill; it is a vital survival skill in today's educational environment. The most successful classrooms are those where this truth is not only recognized but also actively practiced.

What Works: Stories from the Ground

In a second-grade classroom in Texas, "feelings check-ins" are part of the morning attendance. As students place their magnets under "Happy," "Sad," "Worried," or "Tired," the teacher adjusts her tone and pacing accordingly. One day, when more than half the class marks "Worried," the lesson slows down. The storytime book is changed. A group discussion follows—not about reading comprehension, but about courage. Academic content remains, but it is rooted in empathy.

In a Detroit high school, a history teacher dedicates five minutes of "collective quiet" to each class. No instructions. No phones. Just presence. Students say they feel more focused, and office referrals from that classroom have dropped by 30 percent. One student said, "It's the only time in my day I don't feel like I have to perform."

At a community college in New York, a psychology professor introduces a "pause assignment" in the middle of the semester. No grade is given—just one question: What do you need right now to keep going? Responses vary from "I need someone to ask how I'm really doing," to "I need one class where I'm not invisible." These answers aren't just stored in the inbox; the professor updates future lectures to include more discussion, relevance, and care.

None of these practices are complicated, but they require intention. They involve redefining what counts as rigor—one that includes emotional safety as a foundation rather than an afterthought.

Putting the Mosaic Into Motion

It's one thing to talk about leading with emotional integrity, cultural flexibility, and identity agility — it's another to see what it looks like when the lesson plan itself becomes a living example. These moments don't require rewriting an entire curriculum or waiting for perfect circumstances. They happen when an educator chooses to adjust in real time, to meet students where they are without losing sight of where they can go. The following vignettes show the Mosaic Intelligence Method™ woven directly into everyday teaching — across subjects, grade levels, and learning environments — turning the "fog" into a space for connection, trust, and growth.

MOSAIC IN MOTION: A Lesson Plan Moment

During a week when the fog feels thickest, a high school history teacher replaces the planned lecture with a "dual lens" activity.

Emotional integrity: Class begins with a short, honest check-in—students share one word for how they're arriving. The teacher shares their own word too.

Cultural flexibility: Instead of a single historical narrative, students compare two perspectives from different cultures on the same event, discussing how cultural background shapes interpretation.

Identity agility: The teacher alternates between guiding discussion, asking open-ended questions, and stepping back to let students lead. By the end, participation has doubled—not because the fog lifted, but because students felt invited to navigate it together.

MOSAIC IN MOTION: Elementary Classroom

In a 4th-grade math lesson, the teacher notices the room's energy is low after recess.

Emotional integrity: Before starting fractions, students take one minute to share a "high" or "low" from their morning.

Cultural flexibility: Word problems are adapted to reflect a variety of cultural foods and traditions so every student sees something familiar in the examples.

Identity agility: When a student offers an unexpected solution, the teacher pauses the lesson to explore their thinking, showing that there's more than one "right" path to understanding.

By the end, students are leaning forward, not because they love fractions, but because they feel part of the conversation.

> **MOSAIC IN MOTION:**
> **Arts & Dance School**

During a rehearsal week, students arrive distracted and underprepared.

Emotional integrity: Class begins with a brief guided breathing exercise to help dancers ground themselves.

Cultural flexibility: The instructor invites students to choose music from diverse backgrounds, allowing them to connect movement to personal or cultural identity.

Identity agility: Instead of drilling choreography, the teacher splits the class—half practice, half peer feedback—then switches roles. Students still meet skill goals, but they also practice leadership and collaboration.

By the end, even the least prepared students have engaged in the process and contributed to the group's growth.

> **MOSAIC IN MOTION:**
> **Higher Education Seminar**

In a graduate-level sociology course, the professor senses low engagement during a complex theory discussion.

Emotional integrity: The professor pauses and invites students to share one word that describes their mental bandwidth at that moment.

Cultural flexibility: Case studies are swapped for real-time examples from students' own communities, encouraging application across cultural contexts.

Identity agility: The professor shifts from lecturer to facilitator, organizing students into small groups where they lead each other through the theory.

Students leave not only understanding the material better but also feeling ownership over the discussion.

This is what it means to lead through the fog — not around it. Not avoiding, not pretending, not waiting for a "better day." But choosing to engage with the moment as it is, while staying emotionally grounded, culturally responsive, and true to oneself.

This is leadership that doesn't just endure challenges. It turns them into a deeper form of presence—one that teaches, not just facts, but what it truly means to be human.

Lead Anyway Reflection

- When was the last time you noticed your students were mentally or emotionally absent, even when they were physically present?
- How has the emotional fog of recent years affected your teaching or leadership approach?
- What unspoken expectations are you putting on yourself to "perform" when you're genuinely exhausted?
- Where can you create more space for yourself—and your students—to feel, reflect, and reset?
- What would it look like to lead with emotional presence rather than performative energy?

Maybe Mr. Givens didn't fail. Perhaps he was teaching the one lesson his students needed most: that even in the fog, he stayed.

TOOL TO TRY:
Acknowledge the Fog Out Loud

When energy drops in the room, say it: "Today feels heavy—anyone else feel it?" Normalizing emotional climate can shift silence from confusion to shared humanity.

TOOL TO TRY:
Say the Fog Out Loud

When emotional heaviness or distraction is present, name it. "This feels like one of those foggy days—anyone else feel that?" Naming it allows students to re-engage without shame.

CHAPTER 4

Beyond the Label: Seeing Students in Their Full Humanity

The Labels Don't Hold

Jordan was labeled as "at-risk." Mateo had an IEP. Lila was identified as "gifted but defiant." These labels were attached to their files and conveyed a lot on paper. But in the classroom, they only touched the surface.

Jordan was coping with the loss of a sibling while trying to pass chemistry. Mateo's anxiety made it hard to sit still in class, but he was a skilled coder. Lila hid her loneliness behind sarcasm, yet she wrote poetry that could move adults to tears. The forms captured didn't reveal who these students truly were—only how they had been categorized.

"Students are not data points. They are living stories waiting to be read with care."

We live in a time when identity is complex, evolving, and deeply personal. Our students are not just learners; they embody culture, trauma, brilliance, confusion, and hope. If we guide them solely with systems designed for simplicity, we will overlook the richness—and responsibility—of truly understanding who they are.

More Than a Generation

It's tempting to use generational labels like Gen Z, Alpha, or post-pandemic learners. However, no single label can capture the complexity of the students today. This generation is dealing with more psychological issues by age thirteen than many adults experienced during their entire youth. They are growing up in an environment where identity is highly visible yet constantly challenged—both online and in real life.

Many are questioning long-held beliefs about gender, race, family structure, faith, and even reality itself. They are becoming more emotionally fluent even as they grapple with emotional fatigue. They are unafraid to challenge norms but are deeply uncertain about their place in the world. And they bring all of this into the classroom.

If we see today's students through outdated stereotypes—obedient or defiant, high-achiever or low-performing, "good kid" or "troublemaker"—we will fail them because they no longer fit those roles. They are creating entirely new scripts, and the most effective educators aren't threatened by that; they're curious about it.

Cultural Context and Identity Conflict

In every classroom, identity is fluid. A student may speak one language at home and a different one at school. They might present themselves in one way online and another in person. They may dress to fit in but carry internal tensions that few adults ever ask about.

College students often carry the burden of generational expectations—especially first-generation scholars—while trying to find their own voice. Middle schoolers explore gender expression under the intense scrutiny of peer judgment and school policies. Elementary students internalize messages about race, power, and belonging long before they can find the words to express what they feel.

Identity is not a sidebar issue in education. It is the curriculum beneath the curriculum.

And yet, too many educational environments ignore identity until it becomes disruptive. Systems react to the behavior without ever considering the backstory. Teachers are expected to "manage" students without first understanding them. But the truth is simple and urgent: identity is always present—whether or not we acknowledge it.

The **Mosaic Intelligence Method**™ places identity at the heart of educational leadership. Not only student identity but also educator identity. When we lead without recognizing our own emotional states, cultural assumptions, or inherited biases, we unintentionally replicate the very dynamics we seek to challenge.

That's why this method isn't just a set of techniques—it's a transformative framework based on three key practices.

Emotional Integrity

Educators must be honest about who they are, how they feel, and what they carry. Emotional integrity involves modeling self-awareness, not self-denial. It's how we build trust—not through performance, but through presence. Students aren't asking us to be superheroes; they are observing how we handle complexity, how we regulate ourselves, and how we repair when we make mistakes.

Cultural Flexibility

This isn't about celebrating holidays or translating newsletters. Cultural flexibility is about adopting a posture that values complexity over conformity. It involves the willingness to shift our perspective—not just our lesson plans. It encourages us to see the story behind silence, the brilliance in behavior, and the pattern beneath resistance. This kind of leadership listens across differences and adjusts without erasing others.

Identity Agility

In the Mosaic classroom, both students and teachers grow. Identity agility means we recognize that no one is fixed—neither our students nor ourselves. It allows us to grow, adapt, and lead with humility instead of ego. It encourages educators to hold multiple truths simultaneously: that a student can be struggling and brilliant, disruptive and insightful, disengaged and deeply aware. It enables us to change our response depending on what the moment calls for—not what tradition requires.

The Mosaic Intelligence Method™ considers identity not a disruption to handle but the fundamental element used to build transformational education.

This isn't just theoretical.
This is how we teach nowadays.
This is how we lead.

Not with rigid scripts, but with reflective strength. Not with fear of getting it wrong, but with the courage to stay in the conversation.

When we lead with emotional integrity, cultural flexibility, and identity agility, we foster classrooms where students don't just survive school—they thrive and become more authentic versions of themselves.

Beyond Visibility—Toward Understanding

Recognizing a student's pronouns or celebrating cultural holidays is a good first step. However, visibility alone isn't enough. Today's students want to be truly understood. They seek adults who ask questions instead of making assumptions, who embrace complexity rather than demanding simplicity, and who lead with humility rather than certainty.

This doesn't mean that educators need to master every identity marker. It means we must be learners too—willing to listen, willing to get it wrong and try again, and willing to create environments where students don't have to erase themselves just to be accepted.

The identity of our students is changing, and so is our role in educating them effectively.

> **MOSAIC IN ACTION:**
> **The Phone Stayed Down**

During independent work time, Ms. Calder noticed Malik staring into his lap, shoulders hunched. Most teachers would've assumed he was scrolling—and she almost did. But instead of calling him out, she walked over, knelt beside his desk, and asked quietly, "Everything okay?" Malik looked up, eyes glassy. "My uncle passed last night." The phone wasn't a distraction—it was his only link to family back home. She gave him the space to step outside and breathe. She didn't manage behavior that day. She honored grief. Presence shifted everything.

What the Research Says

A 2022 report by the Learning Policy Institute highlighted that culturally responsive education is not just about social justice — it's a key to academic success. When students see their identities reflected and valued in the learning environment, they are more likely to engage, stay committed, and succeed. In higher education, research from the National Survey of Student Engagement indicates that students who report feeling "psychologically safe" in their academic spaces show significantly higher levels of retention, resilience, and relational trust.

The key point is clear: when identity is respected, learning improves. When it is overlooked, resistance increases.

Leadership That Sees Beyond the Surface

As educators and leaders, we must learn to look beyond what students display—and beneath what systems label them. The student who skips your class might be dealing with an invisible disability. The one who never turns on their camera could be experiencing housing insecurity. The student who argues against every rule might have never known safety without control.

Who our students are now is more complex than ever. This means our leadership must be more human, more curious, and more courageous than ever before.

What It Looks Like in Real Life

I remember standing at the front of a classroom in the Middle East, feeling the weight of everything I didn't yet understand. The curriculum was Western, but the students were not. My English felt too fast, and my expectations were too rigid. I had prepared for pedagogy, but I hadn't prepared for translation—not of language, but of culture, identity, and trust.

One student, Amal, sat in the front row every day but never spoke. She was respectful, observant, and silent. I assumed she was disengaged—until one afternoon, after class, she waited until everyone left and said quietly, "I understand everything you say. I'm just not used to being asked to speak my opinion. I didn't know if it was allowed."

That moment changed everything. I stopped designing my lessons for participation as performance. Instead, I focused on creating space for slower reflection. I encouraged writing rather than speaking. I shared parts of my own discomfort with adjusting to the culture—not as a formal lesson but as a bridge.

I realized then what I see everywhere now: when students don't participate, it's not always because they're disengaged—it might be because they've never been invited in on their terms.

Gradually, the classroom changed. Students started sharing stories instead of just answers. They asked questions that went beyond the textbook. They trusted me—not because I knew everything, but because I showed I was willing to learn from them too.

This is what culturally responsive leadership requires: not perfection, but presence. Not control, but curiosity. A willingness to unlearn and relearn in service of creating a space where identity is not just tolerated—but honored.

This understanding was reinforced through my doctoral research, where I examined the fragmentation of identity and cultural dissonance faced by Western educators working in international school systems. Many reported feeling torn between the institutional expectations of their home country and the cultural norms of their host country—often juggling multiple, and sometimes conflicting, identities simultaneously. The emotional effort needed to maintain professional roles while dealing with personal disorientation reflected what many students quietly experience every day.

In my study, themes of belonging, role confusion, and identity negotiation consistently emerged. Educators discussed the tension between adapting to local expectations and remaining true to their core values. What surprised me most was how frequently silence became the chosen survival strategy—both for students and teachers. This silence was not a lack of care but a shield against misinterpretation or emotional risk.

These findings mirror what we see in many classrooms worldwide: identity is active, layered, and depends on context. When leadership overlooks this, disconnection increases. But by leading with emotional literacy and cultural humility, we foster spaces for genuine belonging—where both educators and students can be whole, in growth, and fully present.

What It Looks Like for Me Now

I carry that moment with Amal into every room I enter—whether I'm speaking to educators, training leaders, or writing curriculum across cultures. It reminds me that connection always takes priority over content; that inclusion isn't merely a strategy—it's a stance; and that emotional safety starts with the courage to see others clearly, even when their way of showing up feels unfamiliar.

Now, when I teach, I listen for what isn't being said. I design with flexibility rather than assumptions. I pause more often. I ask more questions. And I resist the urge to interpret silence as apathy or challenge as defiance. I see both as signals—opportunities to lean in, not pull back.

Culturally responsive leadership is no longer just a concept I discuss; it's the guiding framework I embrace—not only in classrooms but also in boardrooms, conversations, and every space where trust isn't assumed but earned like a gift.

As I continue to move forward—as a teacher, leader, and learner—I'm dedicated to creating spaces where identity is not just acknowledged but authentically reflected. Where students don't have to forsake themselves to belong. Where leadership stems not from expertise but from humility.

Whenever I think back to that moment with Amal, I am reminded of the educator I am still becoming—and the kind of leader our students continue to need.

Lead Anyway Reflection

- What assumptions do you have about students based on their labels or behaviors?
- How have your cultural experiences shaped your view of identity in the classroom?
- Where might your leadership or teaching practice accidentally mute or weaken student identity?
- What measures are you implementing to understand the cultural and emotional contexts your students experience every day?
- What does it look like to lead with curiosity instead of control in your current educational setting?

TOOL TO TRY:
Make the Invisible Visible

Start a team meeting this month with a check-in: "What are we carrying that others might not see?" Naming invisible labor—emotional, cultural, logistical—fosters solidarity and lessens silent burnout.

TOOL TO TRY:
Validate Without Fixing

When a colleague shares stress or exhaustion, respond with: "That makes sense. I see how much you're holding." You don't have to solve it—just let them feel seen.

CHAPTER 5

Teacher Burnout Is Not a Badge of Honor

The Moment It Snapped

Ms. Harrell didn't realize how tired she was until she snapped at a student for tapping his pencil. It wasn't loud, and it wasn't even disruptive. But at that moment, it felt like too much. Her voice rose. His eyes widened. The classroom froze.

Later, while sitting in her car, she cried. Not because of what happened—but because she realized it wasn't about the pencil. It was about everything she'd been carrying and pretending not to. The late-night grading. The pressure to differentiate every lesson. The expectation to be both therapist and enforcer. The unanswered emails. The mandatory meetings. The kids who kept slipping through the cracks.

"Exhaustion is not a credential. Your wellness is part of the work."

And the worst part? No one had done anything "wrong." But no one had stepped in, either.

The burnout didn't stem from a single crisis. It resulted from a thousand unseen moments—when support was promised but never delivered, when leadership sent another "check-in survey" but never followed through, and when systems recognized the strain but offered nothing beyond a self-care flyer in the staff lounge.

Ms. Harrell wasn't just tired from the workload.

She was tired from feeling invisible.

This is the quiet truth many educators carry: that burnout often comes not just from what we're expected to do, but from who isn't there when it counts. When administration becomes distant, reactive, or absent, the emotional labor increases. And when no one acknowledges that absence, it becomes another burden teachers quietly learn to accept.

But burnout isn't a rite of passage. It isn't a badge of honor.

And acting like it is only makes the damage worse.

The Culture of Overextension

In education, burnout doesn't happen all at once; it develops gradually. We say yes too often, skip breaks, and just "power through." When the exhaustion becomes obvious, it is labeled as dedication. Teachers who give up everything for their students are praised as heroes, while principals who run on empty are admired for their "tireless leadership." Exhaustion becomes a badge of honor—proof that we care.

But caring isn't the same as falling apart.

When burnout is glorified, it becomes normalized. School culture starts to reward overwork and ignore emotional signals. Leaders who model self-sacrifice unintentionally create environments where rest feels like weakness and boundaries feel like betrayal. Over time, even the most passionate educators begin to question whether they can continue.

Burnout Is Not a Personal Failure

It's easy to think that burnout means you're doing something wrong—that if you just managed your time better or had thicker skin, you wouldn't feel this way. But burnout isn't a sign of failure; it's a sign of imbalance. It's your nervous system raising a red flag, indicating that the numbers don't add up.

You can't keep giving from an empty well. You can't lead others while silently struggling. You can't be the emotional anchor of your classroom if you've detached from your own needs.

This isn't about weakness—it's about capacity. Even the strongest among us have limits. Recognizing those limits doesn't mean you care less; it means you care wisely—for your students and yourself.

These patterns are not just anecdotal. In my doctoral research on Western educators navigating identity and belonging in international school settings, emotional exhaustion emerged as a common theme. Many participants described feeling torn between the roles they were expected to fulfill and the identities they were struggling to uphold. The inability to rest wasn't simply due to workload—it originated from the pressure to constantly prove one's legitimacy in unfamiliar, high-stakes environments. Burnout, I realized, is often the result of identity fragmentation as much as task overload.

Mosaic Moment: Choosing to Leave on Time

Mr. Alston looked at the growing pile of ungraded papers on his desk. It was already past contract hours, and his headache was starting again. For once, he didn't reach for his laptop; instead, he grabbed his keys. "They'll get done," he reminded himself. That night, he took a walk with his daughter and laughed more than he had in weeks. No applause. No gold star. But he showed up to class the next day feeling clearer, calmer, and more connected. That, too, is leadership. That's what it means to honor capacity without apology.

The Research Behind the Burnout

According to a 2022 report from the National Education Association, 55 percent of educators considered leaving the profession earlier than planned due to stress and burnout. Among those who stayed, 86 percent reported high levels of emotional fatigue, with many citing a lack of support and unmanageable workloads as key factors. In higher education, faculty across disciplines report similar trends—especially among adjunct instructors, women, and educators of color, who often carry disproportionate emotional labor without recognition or relief.

These numbers go beyond statistics; they are warnings. Furthermore, they confirm what many educators already sense: the system is taking more than it is giving back.

But the solution isn't to push through; it's to build differently. That starts with redefining our view of leadership—not as depletion in service of others, but as sustainability in service of all.

Redefining What Commitment Looks Like

We need a new way to define commitment—one that respects boundaries, not just sacrifice. One that understands that overextending ourselves isn't a virtue, and that burnout should never be the price of being called "dedicated."

Teachers shouldn't have to prove their worth by the number of hours they stay after school. Principals shouldn't be expected to manage entire buildings without shared vision or support. Professors shouldn't be left to absorb the emotional trauma of their students while navigating institutional silence, unstable leadership, or chronic underfunding.

And yet, in far too many places, that's exactly what's happening.

Educators are often praised for "doing whatever it takes," but left alone when the emotional toll becomes clear. The expectation to give endlessly is seen as professionalism, while the lack of structural support from administration goes unchallenged.

It's not sustainable.

It's not ethical.

And it's not leadership.

Caring deeply must go hand in hand with caring wisely. We can love this work and still say no. We can lead with conviction and still leave on time. We can be available to our students and still refuse to be emotionally drained by systems that overlook our needs.

This is how the profession becomes sustainable again—not through more individual effort, but through collective agreements that prioritize humanity over hustle. Through leadership that recognizes the cost before it turns into a crisis. Through systems that view teachers as whole people—not just service providers.

This is what emotional integrity looks like in action—a key principle of the Mosaic Intelligence Method™. It means we don't sacrifice our wellbeing for strength. We honestly share how we're doing. We set boundaries that protect both the work and the worker.

It also promotes identity agility—the ability to redefine what it means to be a "committed educator" in a world that constantly shifts the goalposts. It enables us to reject the myths of martyrdom and adopt new leadership models rooted in emotional clarity and self-preservation.

And when school culture resists these shifts?

That's when cultural flexibility becomes crucial. Because sometimes, leading wisely involves challenging norms. Sometimes, it means being the first to leave on time—not because you don't care, but because you do. And because others need to see that it's possible.

Redefining commitment is not a betrayal of the profession.

It's what might actually save it.

The Courage to Rest

Rest is not a retreat from leadership; it is a core part of it. When educators take time to pause, they create room for reflection, recalibration, and renewal. When school leaders set boundaries, they enable their teams to protect their well-being. When rest is integrated—not just allowed—it becomes a means of cultural restoration.

Burnout is real, but it doesn't have to happen. Through meaningful conversations, strong leadership, and giving ourselves permission to be human, we can build school cultures where burnout isn't the cost of making an impact and where perseverance doesn't mean suffering.

Small Wins, Big Shifts: What Recovery Really Looks Like

The idea of rest is often misunderstood. People think it means a beach, a plane ticket, or a sabbatical. But for most educators, especially during the school year, those options are rare—not to mention often out of reach. A vacation can offer temporary relief, but daily practices provide lasting resilience.

Sometimes recovery means leaving papers ungraded for one more night and choosing a walk instead. Sometimes it involves taking five minutes of quiet in your car before entering the building. Sometimes it calls for saying no to another committee, even if guilt surfaces. These aren't luxuries; they're boundaries. And they are essential.

I've been stuck in bed grading papers, trying to meet a deadline that only I will remember. I know you've felt it, too. There's a quiet pressure in education to sacrifice our health for the sake of the mission. But burnout isn't a badge of honor, and neglecting ourselves isn't a leadership tactic.

When I lived in Saudi Arabia, I would go on long weekend bike rides—15 to 20 miles at a time along the desert trails. There was something healing about the rhythm of movement, the solitude, and the physical exertion without performance. It became my reset. In Dubai, I joined the local cycling community and rode four to six times a week, often before the city was fully awake. Those early rides weren't just workouts—they were sacred acts of preservation. They reminded me that I was a whole person, not just a professional role.

Not everyone will be a cyclist. That isn't the point. The goal is to find what works for you—and make it a priority. Make it non-negotiable. If you wait until the system says it's okay to rest, you'll burn out long before you get permission.

Leadership isn't always about being in control. Sometimes, it's about knowing when to step back, so you can keep showing up—whole, present, and healthy.

Lead Anyway Reflection

- When was the last time you felt emotionally or physically drained by your work—and did you allow yourself to notice it?
- What signs of burnout are you overlooking right now, and why?
- In what ways have you linked exhaustion to dedication in your leadership or teaching role?
- How might your school culture shift if rest, boundaries, and recovery were truly respected instead of silently resented?
- What does it mean to lead from wholeness instead of depletion?

TOOL TO TRY:
Practice Micro-Honesty

When you're asked "How are you?"—answer with one truthful word. Not your whole life story, just enough to stop the performance spiral and reconnect to yourself.

TOOL TO TRY:
Teach Through the Imperfect

When something goes wrong in class, calmly acknowledge it: "That didn't land how I hoped—let's adjust." Students learn more from seeing repair than watching you pretend it's fine.

PART II

Leading Beyond the Job Description

DR. KARISSA THOMAS

The Unwritten Expectations That Define the Role

There is the job you were hired for— and then there is the job you actually do.

Officially, you might be a teacher, assistant principal, or professor. Your title comes with a description: deliver instruction, manage learning environments, track progress, and support student development. However, anyone who has spent even a week in the field knows this list barely scratches the surface.

Today's educators serve as mentors, mediators, first responders, emotional anchors, and sometimes the only stable adult presence in a student's life. The job description doesn't include holding space for trauma, absorbing the tension of broken systems, or navigating parent meetings that often feel more like negotiations. It doesn't explain how to regulate your own nervous system while de-escalating a student's. It also doesn't prepare you for absorbing frustration from colleagues, confusion from students, and constant changes from leadership.

These are the unspoken expectations of the job—and the real stage where leadership happens.

This part of the book isn't about the job you were trained for. It's about the job you've grown into — the one where emotional presence, trust in relationships, and cultural understanding matter more than policies or procedures. The one where your title might say educator, but your impact speaks loudly.

This also builds directly on my own doctoral research, which examined the identity development and emotional labor of Western educators working in international schools in the UAE. What emerged was a pattern of deep dissonance—between who teachers were and who they were expected to be. Many reported navigating identity fragmentation, cultural tension, and a quiet erosion of belonging. These were not simply professional challenges; they were personal fractures. And they are not isolated. Across both local and global contexts, educators are carrying invisible weight that transcends curriculum or job scope.

This is also where the Mosaic Intelligence Method™ extends its influence. Beyond the official job description, there's a deeper purpose:

to lead with emotional integrity, respond with cultural flexibility, and adapt with identity agility in real time. These aren't just leadership qualities—they're essential survival skills in a profession where expectations change daily.

The upcoming chapters delve into the unseen work of leadership. They emphasize the pressure, complexity, and influence of leading from the middle, from the margins, or from within a system that often views you as replaceable. Most importantly, they remind you: leadership is not a promotion — it's a stance. Some of the most impactful leaders are those quietly shaping the future, without recognition, beyond the bullet points of their job description.

This is where we lead anyway.

CHAPTER 6

When the System Doesn't See You

Invisible in Plain Sight

Mrs. Young arrived early every day. She unlocked the front doors of the school before the custodian clocked in. She handled morning duty, coached the step team, mentored new teachers, and coordinated every community event. Her title? Classroom teacher.

Despite her influence, she was seldom recognized. Decisions were made without her input. Leadership meetings happened around her, not with her. When the district sent a survey asking about leadership morale, she almost laughed. What leadership? I'm not seen as that.

"Just because your work is invisible doesn't mean it's insignificant."

But she was a leader. She just wasn't recognized as one. Like many educators, she led beyond her title—impacting culture, earning trust, and carrying emotional weight that went unspoken and unpaid.

Remaining unseen in a system that demands so much from you is more than frustrating; it's draining.

DR. KARISSA THOMAS

The Silent Labor of Leadership

There's the leadership people see—and then there's the kind that keeps everything running smoothly: the hallway conversations that ease tension before it rises, the check-in texts to a struggling colleague, and the moments after class when a student stays behind to become your emotional lifeline.

This type of leadership isn't about a stipend or title. It comes from an inner compass that says, "I can't ignore what's happening around me." It originates from a sense of responsibility to the people in the room—not just to the content on the board.

It often goes unnoticed.

When systems focus on performance metrics, data walls, and compliance checklists, relational leadership becomes hidden. Yet, it is this unseen labor that determines whether a school culture falls apart or stays strong. The tension is real: you're doing the work but not being empowered to lead.

Underestimated and Overextended

Educators who lead from within—without formal authority—are often both underestimated and overextended. They are trusted by students, relied on by colleagues, and stretched by leadership. Yet, they are excluded from decisions, overlooked for promotions, or told to "just focus on your classroom."

This is especially true for educators of color, women, LGBTQ+ faculty, and paraprofessionals—those whose leadership is often relational rather than formal. Their influence is felt but not officially recognized. Their wisdom is used but not credited. Their presence creates space, but the space rarely accommodates them in return.

This causes emotional whiplash: feeling essential to your community while being unseen by your institution.

When Admin Is Absent, Reactive, or Unsafe

Sometimes the hardest part of leading from within is knowing that the very people meant to protect, support, or guide you have vanished—or worse, become a source of harm.

There's the administrator who only surfaces during observations or conflicts. The one who sends motivational emails but avoids real conversations.

The one who publicly champions teacher wellbeing but privately retaliates when boundaries are set.

This absence isn't just logistical—it's emotional.

When administrators are reactive instead of responsive, or invisible when presence is most needed, educators start to internalize a disturbing message: you're on your own.

This silence leads to erosion.

Not just of morale—but of trust, courage, and the will to remain.

The **Mosaic Intelligence Method**™ identifies this as a leadership trauma—an erosion of relational trust within hierarchical systems. And it provides tools to navigate it clearly.

> **Emotional integrity** helps you identify the cost of being unsupported—without making it seem normal.

> **Cultural flexibility** reminds you that others might also be experiencing harm, even if it appears different.

> **Identity agility** allows you to lead on your own terms—rather than following outdated or broken authority structures.

We can't always change who's above us leading. But we can become architects of spaces that refuse to mimic their silence.

Mosaic Moment: A Pause in the Hallway

As the final bell rang, Ms. Barlow noticed a student lingering near the lockers, shoulders tense, eyes distant. No referral. No outburst. Just silence. Instead of rushing to her next duty, she paused. "You okay?" she asked softly. The student didn't respond right away, but the tension eased. That 30-second check-in didn't make the data wall. It didn't change test scores. But it reminded a child they mattered. That's emotional integrity in action—seeing someone before they fall through the cracks.

What the Research Shows

A 2023 study published in Educational Administration Quarterly found that non-positional teacher leaders—those without formal titles—play a crucial role in shaping school climate, mentoring peers, and bridging gaps between students and administration. However, their contributions are often overlooked in leadership evaluations and professional development programs.

In higher education, adjunct faculty consistently report feeling excluded from institutional planning, even though they are the primary instructors for most undergraduates. This invisibility causes lower job satisfaction and leads to higher turnover among those who do the emotional labor of student engagement without structural support.

These findings closely match my own doctoral research, which explored the identity development and emotional labor of Western educators teaching in international school settings. Many participants described the disconnect between their visible contributions and their institutional invisibility. They bore the emotional weight of leadership without formal recognition—often while navigating cultural complexities, professional marginalization, and identity fragmentation. In these environments, the lack of acknowledgment wasn't just disappointing; it became a barrier to feeling like they belonged. Over time, many started to internalize the system's silence, doubting their legitimacy despite their real impact.

The research clearly shows that leadership is happening everywhere—but systems continue to prioritize visibility over real value.

Adjunct in the Margins

Javier had been working as an adjunct faculty member for seven years—across five different campuses, without benefits or voting rights in department decisions. He was known for mentoring underrepresented students and hosting inclusive office hours in the student café. Still, his name never appeared on committee rosters or policy memos. The emotional toll wasn't just exhaustion; it was erasure. Javier's story reminds us: invisible labor doesn't mean invisible impact. But it does mean we need systems that recognize and support the people working on the margins.

Choosing to Lead Anyway

When the system doesn't recognize you, you face a choice: step back or lead regardless.

Leading doesn't mean tolerating injustice. It means refusing to let the system's blindness define your worth. It means setting your own impact standards—not by who praises you, but by who trusts you, who grows because of you, and who dares to lead after seeing you.

It also involves seeking alignment, discovering spaces where your talents are recognized, fostering relationships where your presence is valued, and creating chances where you don't just survive within the system but start to reshape it.

Being unseen is painful. However, it can also bring clarity. When the applause fades, what's left is purpose.

And that purpose? That's your power.

This is where the **Mosaic Intelligence Method**™ speaks directly to the core of unseen leadership. It reminds us that:

Emotional integrity isn't about recognition. It's a quiet decision to stay true to your values, even when no one is watching.

Cultural flexibility allows you to lead in complex, fragmented environments—respecting their diversity without becoming overwhelmed.

Identity agility lets you define leadership on your own terms—not through hierarchy or visibility, but through the genuine impact of your presence.

When systems overlook you, the Mosaic Intelligence Method™ helps you see yourself clearly.
And that clarity? It's not just a survival skill—it's a leadership strategy.

What Janitors Taught Me About Leadership

This kind of leadership isn't exclusive to teachers or administrators.
We've all known janitors who have stepped up as true leaders—quiet leaders.
As a child, I remember the janitors who would offer a quiet word of encouragement or help clean up more than just spills—they cleaned up fear, frustration, and sometimes the emotional mess that no one else noticed. In elementary school and again in high school, they were there—steady, kind, and present. They saw us when others didn't. They protected us in ways that the rulebooks didn't cover.
Now, as an educator, I see even more clearly how crucial their presence is. Janitors are often the first to arrive and the last to leave. They observe more than we do. They notice when a student is sitting alone in the hallway. They step in to de-escalate situations before they escalate. They help carry the emotional climate of a school without ever being asked—and without ever receiving credit.
Their leadership is powerful but quietly suppressed. Still, they lead anyway.
This has influenced how I see my own role. To me, leadership isn't about a title; it's about attitude, presence, and the people who lead when no one is watching, when no one is applauding, and when no one has formally asked them to do so.
So when I think about what it means to lead anyway, I think of them. I think of all the "unofficial leaders" who keep schools human. The ones who may never speak at a faculty meeting, but whose actions

speak volumes every day. And I ask myself: *How can I lead like that? How can I honor their example—not with sympathy, but with solidarity?*

Because if we want to change our school cultures, we don't need more titles; we need more truth. We must recognize that leadership has always been happening—quietly, steadily, and often from the margins.

And if we pay attention to those who have been leading all along, we might remember how to lead with integrity, not ego. With service, not status. With presence, not performance.

That is the kind of leadership that sustains both schools and souls. That is the kind we can trust.

And it's the kind that every student, educator, and community deserves.

Lead Anyway Reflection

- Have you ever felt that your leadership was overlooked or undervalued because of your title or position?
- What parts of your influence go unnoticed, and how have you managed to affirm yourself despite that?
- Where are you still waiting for permission to lead, and what would change if you granted it to yourself?
- How can you boost your visibility without sacrificing your integrity?
- What would it look like to build a culture—at your school or institution—where invisible leadership is recognized rather than ignored?

TOOL TO TRY:
Affirm Unseen Labor

At the end of the week, text or tell a colleague, "I saw how you handled that situation—you made it look easy, but I know it wasn't." Hidden leadership needs visible affirmation.

TOOL TO TRY:
Make Space to Be Seen

Choose one space this week—such as a staff meeting, parent call, or class discussion—and share a leadership moment you're proud of. Don't minimize your impact. Visibility is essential for sustainability.

CHAPTER 7

Leading from Wholeness: Reimagining School Leadership for a New Era

The Principal Who Sat Down

Mr. Daniels had always been a strong presence—visible, decisive, respected. However, after a particularly turbulent school year marked by teacher turnover, parent outrage, and student disengagement, something in him shifted. During a heated staff meeting, instead of pushing through the agenda, he sat down in front of his team and said, "I don't have the answers. But I know we can't lead like this anymore."

"Real leadership isn't control—it's connection with responsibility."

The room grew silent. They didn't see weakness; they saw humanity.

That moment transformed everything. For the first time, the staff viewed their leader not as a boss but as a teammate. He didn't give up responsibility; he shared respect.

Leadership in education has traditionally been linked to authority—top-down orders, strict limits, and high expectations. However, the leaders making an impact today are not just authoritative. They are relational and emotionally in tune. They lead with clarity and compassion, not control.

The landscape has shifted; leadership must shift too.

From Command to Connection

The traditional model of school leadership emphasized efficiency, order, and compliance. Principals were expected to maintain structure, protect test scores, and enforce rules. Assistant principals were responsible for keeping discipline. College administrators were tasked with reaching enrollment goals. There was little emphasis on complexity, vulnerability, or context.

But today's students—and today's educators—are not responding to command and control. They are responding to connection: to leadership that sees them, listens to them, and leads with, not just over, them.

The most effective leaders today are those who move through buildings with emotional presence, not just a clipboard; who lead restorative conversations instead of disciplinary hearings; and who check in before they check boxes.

The shift is evident: leadership in education is no longer about formal authority; it's about relational influence.

The Pressure to Perform

Despite increasing awareness of relational leadership, many school leaders still feel limited by performance metrics. They are judged by test scores, compliance checks, and teacher evaluations. College department heads are evaluated on credit-hour completion and faculty productivity. There's little chance to lead differently when your metrics are designed for uniformity.

So, leaders tend to overcompensate. They micromanage, hide doubt, and stay busy instead of being present. This happens because appearing strong often feels safer than showing vulnerability.

But here's the truth: the strongest leaders aren't those who have all the answers. They are those who know how to build teams that ask the right questions. They don't lead by image—they lead through trust.

> **MOSAIC IN ACTION:**
> **When Presence Becomes the Strategy**

During a tense moment at a high school in transition, the assistant principal noticed a veteran teacher growing increasingly withdrawn. Instead of emailing a formal observation or adding another item to the PD calendar, she sat with the teacher during lunch and simply said, "You don't seem like yourself lately. How are you—really?"

That 15-minute check-in didn't resolve everything, but it made a difference. The teacher later said, "That was the first time in months I felt seen—not evaluated."

Emotional integrity was evident in the assistant principal's willingness to pause performance expectations and focus on human connection.

Cultural flexibility showed in how she adapted her leadership tone to suit the situation, instead of applying a one-size-fits-all approach.

Identity agility was demonstrated through her quiet confidence—not needing to "fix," but simply to be present.

This wasn't scheduled, but it turned out to be the most crucial leadership move of the week.

What the Research Says

A 2021 report by the Wallace Foundation found that effective school leadership—especially in high-stress, under-resourced environments—is most strongly linked to three factors: emotional intelligence, relational trust, and distributed leadership practices. Schools with high principal visibility but low staff trust experienced higher turnover rates. In schools where leaders practiced vulnerability and relational accountability, staff retention improved, teacher morale increased, and student growth was boosted.

In higher education, similar results came from a 2022 study in The Review of Higher Education, showing that academic departments with "empathetic leadership cultures" had significantly better faculty collaboration and student satisfaction—regardless of institutional rank or funding.

My own doctoral research confirmed this from a different angle. Examining educators across international and cross-cultural settings, I discovered that many faced significant identity fragmentation and emotional dissonance—especially when expected to lead without sufficient recognition or support. These educators often performed invisible labor, continually balancing cultural adaptation, institutional politics, and internal conflicts about who they were allowed to be in their roles. Despite these struggles, many still managed to lead effectively—not by conforming but by leading from their whole selves.

Their success wasn't about charisma or compliance — it was rooted in emotional integrity, cultural adaptability, and identity agility. These insights formed the foundation for the Mosaic Intelligence Method™, a framework designed not just to teach leadership but to acknowledge the complexity of becoming a leader in spaces that might not always recognize you.

Making the Shift

Reimagining leadership doesn't mean abandoning standards; it means leading with soul through them. It involves shifting from enforcement to engagement, from supervision to support, and from managing people to understanding them.

This type of leadership is slower—but deeper. It is less reactive—but more sustainable. It allows teams to breathe, students to trust, and schools to become places where learning—and healing—can happen.

You don't have to lead the way your mentors did. You aren't required to copy the systems that influenced you. Instead, you can lead differently. This approach allows you to redefine what leadership in education truly means — not just for your building, but for everyone within it.

Leading from Wholeness

This is where the **Mosaic Intelligence Method**™ comes in— not just as another leadership model to memorize, but as a framework to help you become more of who you truly are.

My research affirms—and my ongoing experience confirms— that educational leadership must adapt to address the emotional, cultural, and identity complexities of this time. The challenges we encounter are not just logistical or instructional; they are fundamentally human. They demand leaders who can navigate uncertainty, show up with confidence, and remain true to themselves even when systems fail to support them.

This insight resulted in the creation of the **Mosaic Intelligence Method**™, a leadership framework based on three core capacities:

> **Emotional Integrity:** The ability to lead with emotional honesty, rather than just performance—recognizing your feelings, managing them under pressure, and demonstrating authenticity in settings that often reward silence.

> **Cultural Flexibility:** The ability to lead across differences— with empathy, adaptability, and a willingness to listen deeply even when it becomes uncomfortable.

> **Identity Agility:** The ability to evolve and reimagine yourself as a leader through different seasons of change, without being bound by outdated roles or expectations.

In my research with educators worldwide in high-pressure environments, the most effective leaders weren't just technically skilled. They were emotionally present. They were culturally aware. And most importantly, they were rooted in who they were—not just what they were trained to do.

This method isn't about taking on more. It's about reconnecting with your core. It provides a map back to yourself, especially when work pulls you in a thousand directions.

As an educator, I've learned that when I lead with emotional honesty, cultural awareness, and a genuine relationship with my evolving identity, I don't just survive—I grow. I become more grounded, more generous, and better equipped to handle the complexity around me because I'm no longer fragmented inside.

The **Mosaic Intelligence Method**™ is more than a checklist. It's a lived practice. It's a recalibration. It's a return to integrity.

Because the truth is—you already hold everything this method reveals. It's not about becoming something new. It's about uncovering what's already within you, beneath the noise.

And the more we lead with that kind of authenticity, the more space we create for others to do the same.

That's where transformation begins—not with control, but with connection.

Not from burnout, but from wholeness.

What It Looks Like in Real Life

In real life, the Mosaic Intelligence Method™ shows up when an educator pauses after a disciplinary referral—not to punish more quickly, but to ask better questions. It's the principal who notices a teacher withdrawing during staff meetings and checks in—not with judgment, but with curiosity. It's the professor who redesigns their syllabus to reflect the diverse cultural backgrounds of their students—not to meet a quota, but to create belonging on purpose.

It also appears that the educator who values their own identity—who no longer separates their language, culture, or story to fit institutional standards. It's the teacher who openly shares their own learning journey, not as a performance, but as a way to demonstrate emotional integrity. It's the school leader who moves from control to collaboration, not because it's fashionable, but because they have realized that true power is shared, not hoarded.

The Mosaic Intelligence Method™ isn't a leadership style you choose. It's who you become when you shed the need to perform and let your wholeness lead. It's how you approach complexity with compassion. It's how you go beyond simply surviving the system and start shaping it—with presence, courage, and humanity.

A Final Reflection

I once met a school leader who quietly transformed her entire building—not by issuing mandates, but by setting an example. She didn't run the loudest professional development sessions or dominate meeting agendas. Instead, she remembered birthdays and wrote handwritten notes to every staff member. She met weekly with students who had been suspended—not to lecture them, but to ask about their lives. By June, referrals decreased, morale improved, and teachers who had planned to leave decided to stay.

When I asked her what had changed, she responded, "I stopped managing. I started listening. I gave them what I needed most—permission to matter."

That is true leadership. That is the result of leading from a place of wholeness.

And that is what the next era of education requires.

Lead Anyway Reflection

- What leadership habits have you inherited that no longer match the realities of your school or institution?
- How frequently do you lead through presence instead of performance?
- What does vulnerability in leadership mean to you—and what has prevented you from embracing it?
- Where can you shift from managing others to promoting their growth?
- If you could redefine leadership in a single sentence based on your values— not your job description—what would it be?

TOOL TO TRY:
Reflect, Then Respond

When student behavior triggers you, pause before reacting. Ask: "Is this about them, or is this touching something in me?" Respond from reflection, not reaction.

TOOL TO TRY:
Share a Mirror Moment

Once a week, tell your students: "This moment made me think about my own learning journey." Modeling reflection encourages them to see learning as part of their identity—not just as content.

Mosaic Intelligence in Practice

Leading Beyond Titles

At the core of this book is a leadership model tailored for today's complex educational settings. The **Mosaic Intelligence Method**™ provides a values-driven framework for leading with compassion in high-pressure situations. It isn't a program; it's a stance—a way of presenting yourself—rooted in your identity and responsive to the needs of the moment.

This approach encourages educators, school leaders, and faculty to increase their impact by leading from the inside out. It focuses on the human experience—not as an afterthought, but as a key driver of meaningful, sustainable change. Mosaic leaders don't wait for permission to lead; they lead through presence, purpose, and self-awareness.

Emotional Integrity

Leading through self-awareness, emotional literacy, and grounded presence.

Emotional integrity involves being honest about your feelings, clear about your needs, and brave enough to lead openly. It's about staying grounded, even in emotionally intense situations. Educators with emotional integrity don't avoid discomfort—they confront it with care. They manage their own nervous systems, show vulnerability with strength, and refuse to lead through denial, overcontrol, or burnout.

Cultural Flexibility

Responding thoughtfully across differences.

Cultural flexibility is the ability to lead in diverse, layered environments with respect, curiosity, and courage. It respects identity without demanding sameness. It listens before it responds. It creates space for nuance, disagreement, and healing. Leaders with cultural flexibility can hold multiple perspectives without breaking down, and they actively build trust across generational, racial, linguistic, and cultural boundaries. This pillar reduces harm and fosters space for restorative connection.

Identity Agility

Staying grounded and adaptable as you grow.

Identity agility is the ability to adapt without losing oneself. It helps educators and leaders stay true to their values while managing systemic change, shifting expectations, and personal growth. Leaders with identity agility aren't stuck in old stories or roles—they make space for growth. They lead from a strong relationship with their own evolving story and extend that same understanding to others.

When practiced together, these three capacities form the foundation for emotionally intelligent, culturally responsive, and personally sustainable leadership.
They enable us to lead not just from our role—but from our roots.
True leadership today demands not only strategy but also soul.

CHAPTER 8

Hard Conversations in Fragile Spaces

The Meeting That Went Too Quiet

It started with good intentions. The assistant principal invited staff to share concerns about student behavior. Instead, she got silence. Eyes down. Arms crossed. Tension hung thick in the room.

Finally, one teacher spoke. "We're doing everything we can. Maybe if leadership showed up in the halls, you'd see what we're dealing with."

The air shifted, but no one responded. The meeting pressed on, yet something had fractured—not because the teacher told the truth, but because the space wasn't ready to handle it.

"Hard truths don't break relationships. Avoiding them does."

Hard conversations are essential in education. However, if we don't know how to handle them—if we approach them without emotional readiness, safety, or self-awareness—they can cause more harm than good.

Unspoken Truths and Emotional Landmines

Schools are full of emotional landmines: race, equity, discipline, bias, burnout, identity, and power. These aren't just abstract issues; they are real, lived experiences. When we avoid naming them, they don't go away—they stay hidden underground.

Staff meetings grow tense. Hallways split apart. Passive resistance takes the place of open conversation. What is left unsaid gets played out in policies, classrooms, and culture.

In my doctoral research, educators—especially those in international and cross-cultural environments—frequently mentioned the exhaustion of managing unresolved emotional tension while trying to stay professional. They explained how institutional avoidance of "hard" topics created divisions in staff cohesion and left many feeling unsupported or invisible during moments that called for courageous leadership.

The challenge isn't just what we discuss—it's how we do it. In fragile school ecosystems, truth must be handled with care. Not with fear. Not with shame. But with enough emotional grounding that we don't fall apart under the weight of honesty.

Conflict as a Mirror

Conflict doesn't always mean something is wrong. Sometimes, it shows that something is being revealed. Our discomfort can signal that we're facing real issues—things that need to be dealt with, not ignored.

A veteran teacher might react defensively to a new DEI initiative, not out of hatred, but from fear of being shamed. A student's outburst in class might not be disrespect; it could be trauma surfacing when they feel misunderstood. An administrator's silence might not show apathy; it could reflect a lack of language to describe what they know needs to change.

What we call resistance is usually unprocessed emotion. Additionally, those we label as difficult people are frequently wounded individuals—just like us.

This emotional undercurrent—what I identified in my research as "hidden identity labor"—often lies beneath the surface of school dynamics. Teachers are not just reacting to policy or pressure; they're responding to deeper questions of identity, value, and emotional safety. And when these internal tensions go unacknowledged, conflict becomes more than a conversation—it becomes a reflection of institutional fragmentation.

Creating Spaces That Can Hold the Truth

The goal of difficult conversations isn't to win; it's to understand. It's to expand our collective ability to stay present when things get serious. That involves setting norms, clarifying intentions, allowing silence, and owning missteps.

Courageous conversations need structure and emotional skill. Rushing them, centering our egos, or confusing honesty with aggression can cause more harm than healing. But when we approach with curiosity, accountability, and care, even difficult moments can foster trust.

The safest spaces aren't the quietest; they're the ones where people feel free to speak up, even when the stakes are high.

What the Research Shows

A 2023 case study published in Educational Leadership found that schools with regular, well-facilitated equity discussions saw measurable increases in staff morale, student belonging, and team cohesion. The key? Psychological safety combined with consistent leadership modeling. When leaders created space for vulnerability—especially their own—others followed.

My dissertation confirmed these findings. In interviews with educators in global and high-pressure environments, participants consistently expressed the need for more than procedural fairness—they desired emotional fairness. They wanted spaces where honesty didn't cost them inclusion, where naming discomfort didn't lead to retaliation, and where their leadership wasn't dismissed the moment it made others uncomfortable.

On the other hand, institutions that made performative inclusion statements without genuine relational effort faced more internal conflict, less trust, and higher turnover—especially among staff from marginalized backgrounds. The message was clear: without emotional safety, even the most polished policy is just an act.

And so the question arises:

What happens when administrators respond to honesty with defense?

What if speaking the truth results in being silenced, penalized, or subtly pushed out?

The truth is unsettling: that's not a Mosaic culture.

That's a culture of fear disguised as progress.

This Is Why the Mosaic Intelligence Method™ Matters

The Mosaic Intelligence Method™ is not built for perfect conditions.

It's meant for moments just like this.

When the room becomes tense.

When leadership pulls back instead of engaging. When authenticity feels dangerous, but silence feels heavier.

This approach is not a script. It's a stance.

Emotional integrity enables you to speak clearly and confidently—even when others go silent. It keeps you rooted in truth without making you confrontational.

Cultural flexibility helps you stay present when others project discomfort or confusion. It reminds you that tension doesn't mean failure — it means friction is finally visible.

Identity agility enables you to lead from within, not by seeking permission. It helps you navigate challenging spaces without losing yourself in the process.

You might not always be able to change the institution, but you can lead in a way that refuses to replicate harm.

You can hold space for dialogue that extends without breaking. You can choose to stay gentle in your humanity while fierce in your clarity.

That is the true essence of leadership—not only facilitating difficult conversations but also embodying them.

The Real Work of Leading Through Tension

If you are an educator, you will face conflict. If you are a leader, you will have conversations that others avoid. And if you are committed to healing school culture, you will need to stay present in emotionally charged environments that demand more than just effective facilitation—they demand inner work.

The true essence of leadership isn't about sidestepping tough conversations; it's about making space for them without diminishing yourself or others in the process.

It means being able to say: "I don't have all the answers, but I'm here for the dialogue." and truly mean it.

Mosaic Moves for Hard Conversations

Three Ways to Lead Through Conflict with the Mosaic Intelligence Method™

1. Emotional Integrity: Ground Yourself Before Speaking

Before engaging in a charged conversation, identify what you're feeling—without judgment. Are you anxious? Protective? Frustrated? Being grounded in emotional truth helps you speak with clarity rather than reactivity.

Try saying:
"This is a difficult topic, and I want to approach it with care. I'm noticing what's coming up for me as we talk."

2. Cultural Flexibility: Listen Beneath the Surface

Assume there's more to the story than what's being said. People bring layered histories into every conversation. Cultural flexibility helps you pause assumptions and stay curious—even when you feel challenged.

Try asking:

"Can you tell me more about what that experience was like for you?"

or

"How is this landing for you?"

3. Identity Agility: Stay Grounded, Not Rigid

Conflict often threatens identity—especially if we feel accused or misunderstood. Identity agility lets you adjust your stance without losing your core self. You don't need to defend who you are—you can stand confidently in it.

Try reflecting:

"This challenges how I've seen myself as a leader. I want to sit with that and learn from it."

Remember:

The goal is not to win the conversation.

The goal is to stay present, stay human, and keep the door open to growth.

What It Looks Like in Real Life

At a diverse urban high school in Texas, tensions had been building for months. A group of students expressed concerns about the lack of representation in the curriculum. Staff meetings were tense; some teachers felt targeted, while others stayed quiet. The principal, Ms. Alvarez, understood that the issue went beyond just a reading list—it was about trust.

Instead of issuing a district-approved "diversity plan," she did something smaller—but braver. She called a voluntary after-school dialogue and began not with policy, but with presence. She started by sharing her own discomfort, admitting she had avoided these conversations for years out of fear of saying the wrong thing. Then she asked, "What have you needed from leadership that you haven't received?"

Initially, there was silence. Then, one teacher spoke, then another. The hour went by, and no one left.

What followed were not perfectly run equity sessions. They were messy, emotional, and genuine. But week by week, the room became more honest. People laughed. Some cried. Staff started to reflect differently—not just about race and identity, but about how they showed up for each other. One teacher later said, "I didn't need a policy—I needed to know I could say something and still be safe."

Within the year, student feedback improved, referrals decreased, and faculty members who had planned to leave decided to stay — not because everything was fixed, but because something had shifted. They had a leader who didn't just assign tasks; she committed fully, imperfectly, and honestly.

That's what embodied leadership is: not a checklist, but a choice repeated again and again.

MOSAIC IN ACTION:
A Mosaic Moment from the Field

During a staff circle at an international school, a teacher of color shared how exhausting it was to constantly represent their culture in every diversity conversation. They weren't angry—but they were weary. Instead of defending themselves, the school leader paused and said, "Thank you for saying that. I've relied on your voice too often, and that's not fair. I need to rethink how I've led this."

The room was silent—but this time, in reverence. That moment didn't solve everything, but it opened the door for shared responsibility. That's identity agility in action: the willingness to reflect, not retreat, in the face of discomfort.

Lead Anyway Reflection

- What tough conversation have you been avoiding in your role, and what is the price of that avoidance?
- How do you usually respond to conflict: do you shut down, become defensive, or over-assert?
- What would it look like to create a space where disagreement is expected—but disrespect is not tolerated?
- When have you seen a difficult conversation go well—and what made it successful?
- How might your leadership change if you saw tension as a teacher instead of a threat?

TOOL TO TRY:
Breathe Before You Speak

Before entering a difficult conversation, take a full breath. Then ask yourself: "Am I showing up to win, or to understand?" That breath can make a big difference.

TOOL TO TRY:
Lead with Listening

Begin the next tense dialogue with: "Before I share anything, I want to understand what you're feeling." When people feel heard first, they listen with less defense.

CHAPTER 9

Restoring Culture Without Toxic Positivity

When "We've Got This" Isn't Enough

The posters in the staff lounge displayed messages like "Stay strong" and "Every day is a fresh start." The school newsletter featured a "shout-out corner" along with motivational quotes. During morning announcements, the principal's voice always radiated cheer: "We're going to have a great day, Bulldogs!"

"Accountability without compassion isolates. Compassion without accountability enables. True culture requires both."

But in the teacher workroom, morale was falling apart. A veteran teacher had just resigned mid-year. Another had been out for weeks on medical leave, citing stress. A first-year teacher was barely holding on. Yet, the message stayed the same: smile, push through, stay positive.

The result wasn't motivation—it was resentment. Teachers didn't need cheerleading; they needed honesty. They needed leadership that recognized reality and still guided them forward.

This is the difference between positivity and toxic positivity: the former lifts you up, while the latter erases you.

The Lie That Hurts More Than the Truth

Toxic positivity doesn't always sound fake. Sometimes it sounds like:
"Let's not focus on the negative."
"At least we still have our jobs."
"It could be worse."

These statements aren't always meant to be harmful—but they dismiss genuine experiences.

When educators are overwhelmed, unheard, or grieving systemic dysfunction, forced optimism does not inspire—it invalidates. It suggests there is no room for complexity and no space to feel disappointed, frustrated, or uncertain.

Over time, that erasure becomes cultural. Staff learn to smile through burnout. Students learn to hide anxiety behind performance. Leaders learn to frame problems as "growth opportunities" rather than addressing what's actually broken.

The cost? Emotional disconnect, cultural mistrust, and silent exits.

My dissertation revealed how performative emotional responses by leadership—especially in international and high-pressure school systems—contributed to what many educators called "emotional gaslighting." Faculty were expected to maintain composure and positivity while silently absorbing the weight of shifting mandates, microaggressions, and unsupported trauma. Over time, that contradiction caused emotional numbness and fostered a cultural climate of self-suppression.

Culture Is Not Climate

Culture isn't just the mood of a building. It includes the deep, often unspoken agreements about what is considered safe to say, how people are treated, and what is prioritized. A school might have a fun, spirited week and still have a toxic culture. A campus can hold a DEI workshop while still suppressing identity. A district might celebrate awards but ignore those doing the heaviest emotional work.

Restoring culture means being honest about what has been lost—and what needs rebuilding. It involves moving beyond superficial statements and toward meaningful purpose. It's not about avoiding pain, but acknowledging it. It's not about cheering louder, but listening more deeply.

Culture shifts when people feel secure enough to express their true selves and valued enough to stay.

What the Research Says

A 2021 report from CASEL (Collaborative for Academic, Social, and Emotional Learning) found that staff well-being improves significantly in schools where leadership models emotional honesty. Educators who felt their emotional experiences were validated reported higher job satisfaction, better student relationships, and a greater willingness to collaborate across departments.

On the other hand, schools that focused on "positivity" without fostering relational transparency experienced more signs of emotional withdrawal, burnout, and conflict avoidance among staff. The lesson? Climate initiatives lacking cultural depth and emotional safety tend to fail.

My own research reflected this. Educators often describe their emotional labor as invisible—necessary but overlooked. One participant explained it this way: "They tell us to be resilient, but they don't ask what's broken. They celebrate the surface and ignore the root."

What rebuilds school culture isn't nonstop cheer—it's steady care.

At the same time, it's crucial to recognize that many school leaders—principals, deans, department chairs—are under immense pressure themselves. Some are dealing with mandates they didn't create, expectations they can't fulfill, and emotional demands that go beyond their training or capacity. They, too, are human. They, too, often feel invisible.

The goal of this framework is not to shift burnout from teachers to administrators. It's to break the burnout cycle altogether—by changing how we define leadership, how we model wellness, and how we structure relational accountability at every level of the system.

The Mosaic Intelligence Method™ is relevant for both administrators and classroom teachers. Since wholeness isn't a luxury for those with fewer responsibilities — it's a fundamental for every leader and a necessity for every school.

This is where the **Mosaic Intelligence Method™** becomes practical — not just as a leadership philosophy, but as an operational shift.

Emotional integrity allows leaders to speak the truth without shame or fear.

Cultural flexibility enables a variety of ways to express stress, grief, and resilience—without judgment.

Identity agility enables us to go beyond role-based performance and engage with the full complexity of ourselves—and our colleagues.

When these capacities are integrated into leadership practice, school culture shifts from fragile to resilient.

Leading with Authentic Hope

Hope and honesty are not opposites. In fact, when paired together, they build the most sustainable form of leadership. Hope says: "I still believe something better is possible." Honesty says: "And I'm not going to pretend we're already there."

Restoring culture starts with identifying what has been lost: trust, time, bandwidth, and perhaps belief in the system. But it doesn't stop there. It involves making decisions that uphold dignity, creating feedback loops that actually close, and fostering leadership moments that replace silence with transparency and isolation with invitation.

It doesn't mean we stop celebrating; it means we stop acting and start creating something genuine.

What It Looks Like in Real Life

At a small rural middle school, staff burnout had become almost unavoidable. Every Friday, the principal sent motivational emails—quotes about perseverance, colorful emojis, reminders to "keep pushing." Yet inside the building, morale was declining. Teachers felt isolated. Planning periods went silent. No one wanted to admit how much they were struggling.

Then one morning, during a faculty meeting, the assistant principal stood up and did something unexpected. She closed her laptop, took a deep breath, and said, "I'm tired. Not the kind of tired that sleep fixes—but the kind that comes from carrying too much and pretending it's fine." There was a long pause. Then someone whispered, "Me too."

That single moment shattered something within.

In the following weeks, the leadership team made space—not just for planning but for being present. One hallway became a "reset zone" where staff could sit quietly or check in with each other. They replaced forced positivity challenges with optional wellness lunches. They invited staff to anonymously share what they needed most—and then followed through on what they could.

There were still tough days, but the culture changed. Teachers stopped hiding their exhaustion and began asking for help—and offering it. Gradually, hope came back. Not the flashy kind, but the real kind. The kind that says, we see each other now.

That's what it means to lead with emotional honesty: not glossing over struggle, but sitting with it, speaking to it, and still choosing to believe in something better.

> **MOSAIC IN ACTION:**
> A Mosaic Moment from the Field

At a private international school in the UAE, staff were praised often—but were never asked how they were truly coping. One teacher finally broke down in a department meeting and said,

"All these thank-yous mean nothing when we're not okay." The department head didn't defend the school or change the subject. She simply said, "You're right. We've been cheerleading, not caring. That's going to change."

And it did. The next week, a new staff well-being check-in process was introduced—simple but sincere. That's emotional integrity: the courage to prioritize presence over performance.

Lead Anyway Reflection

- How have you observed toxic positivity in your school or institution, and what effect did it have on trust?
- How can you balance motivation and honesty in your leadership or teaching?
- What is one hard truth your team or classroom needs to face?
- Where can you replace superficial cheer with more meaningful relational care?
- How might your leadership evolve if you saw culture not as a "vibe," but as a commitment?

TOOL TO TRY:
Check the Cultural Load

When you notice a student or colleague consistently "representing," ask: "Am I relying on this person to speak for a whole group?" Redistribute voice and validate lived experience.

**TOOL TO TRY:
De-center Your Lens**

During lesson planning, pause and ask: "Whose voices are centered here—and who's missing?" Don't just diversify content. Challenge the default perspective.

PART III

Courageous Classrooms, Brave Leaders

DR. KARISSA THOMAS

Leading With Heart in a Time of Hesitation

There comes a point in every educator's journey when strategy isn't enough—when lesson plans, protocols, and data-driven interventions fall short. What's needed isn't more information but more courage.

Courage to speak up in rooms where silence feels safer.
Courage to teach material others avoid.
Courage to show up when the system provides little support.
Courage to lead from a place of wholeness in a profession that often calls for fragmentation.

Courageous classrooms are not defined by perfect instruction. They are characterized by adults who dare to be honest, emotionally present, and deeply human. These adults resist becoming hardened by the system, even as they learn how to navigate it. They hold space for contradiction—in growth and grief, discipline and dignity, rigor and restoration.

And brave leadership isn't about having all the answers. It's about creating space for complexity without losing your center. It's about modeling for students—and your team—what it means to lead with integrity when the path is unclear and the stakes are high.

This section examines a type of leadership that often goes unnoticed in awards ceremonies or staff meetings—but is deeply transformative. It impacts people, not just programs. It leaves a lasting impression on students and colleagues long after the school bell rings.

The upcoming chapters encourage you to lead despite fatigue, resistance, and fear. Even when it's tough. Even when it's unappreciated. Even when it's not in your job description.

Because the truth is: courage in classrooms doesn't just change learning—it transforms. lives.

At its core, this is what the Mosaic Intelligence Method™ enables us to do:

- To lead with **emotional integrity**, even in moments of discomfort.

- To respond with **cultural flexibility**, especially when tension rises.
- To move with **identity agility**, when everything else is shifting.

This isn't just about resilience. It's about relational leadership—the kind that recognizes people, creates space, and remains grounded when systems falter. It starts when we choose courage over comfort—and presence over performance.

CHAPTER 10

Lead Anyway

The Leader Who Stayed Late for One

Years ago, Mr. Alvarez had already packed up and was halfway to the parking lot when he noticed a student sitting outside the school doors. She was quiet, overlooked, and always alone. She wasn't waiting for a ride or on her phone—just sitting there, head down, burdened with something unspoken.

"Even when the fog doesn't lift—you lead anyway."

He almost kept walking. He had papers to grade, a meeting the next morning, and a home to go back to. But something told him to turn around.

He sat beside her—no questions at first, just a quiet presence. Eventually, she spoke, telling him about the eviction, the silence at home, and the loneliness she had carried unnoticed by everyone else.

He didn't fix her problems that night. But later, in a graduation speech no one expected her to give, she said, "That was the night I decided not to disappear."

That's what true leadership looks like. Not a grand plan. Not a huge effort. Just being present. A moment of clarity and compassion that says: I see you. I'm not in a hurry. You matter enough for me to stay.

DR. KARISSA THOMAS

When No One's Watching

The truth is, most of what educators do will never be recognized, celebrated, or even noticed. You'll check on students no one else observes. You'll support colleagues before they falter. You'll rewrite lessons late at night, show up after personal heartbreak, and maintain boundaries no one trained you to uphold.

This is what it truly means to lead, anyway.

To lead when policies fail you, when systems forget you, when gratitude doesn't come. You lead because something within you refuses to become indifferent.

Real leadership is rarely connected to a title. It's rooted in conviction and expressed through quiet integrity, in making tough decisions without seeking applause, and carrying emotional labor with grace. It is based on your refusal to give up on the people you're called to serve—even when pulling back would be easier.

Why You Matter—Even When It Doesn't Feel Like It

There will be days when you wonder if anything you're doing is making a difference. When students appear disengaged. When your team feels far away. When your body is exhausted and your hope is running low.

Still—you show up.

That's what sticks with them. Students remember how you made them feel, not just what you taught. Colleagues recall your steadiness during chaos. Communities remember the educator who didn't look away.

That's the legacy. Not the metrics, not the titles, not the lines on a resume. The legacy is love—shown through consistency, courage, and presence.

What the Research Says

A longitudinal study from the Search Institute found that students who can name just one adult who "sees, supports, and believes in them" are much more likely to graduate, stay emotionally resilient, and develop healthier identities. Not ten adults. Just one.

In school culture, having a single emotionally attuned educator—whether a teacher, administrator, counselor, or coach—can generate ripple effects. Staff retention increases. Behavior incidents decrease. Psychological safety takes hold in systems that are often impersonal or transactional.

Your presence influences the climate, even when the effect isn't immediately visible or obvious.

This is precisely why the **Mosaic Intelligence Method**™ exists. It's not just a theory—it's a practical approach used by people at every level of the institution.

Emotional integrity allows you to lead with honesty, not just performance—whether you're in the classroom, the front office, or the superintendent's seat.

Cultural flexibility allows you to accept diverse ways of expressing needs, emotions, and identity without judgment.

Identity agility keeps you grounded in who you are, even when your role changes, your capacity is tested, or your influence feels limited.

Leading anyway means showing up as a whole person within a fragmented system—not to bear all the weight alone, but to demonstrate what real leadership is: grounded, attuned, and courageous.

This Is the Work

Leading in any role means accepting that transformation requires time—and that you might not always witness the results of your efforts. But the effort remains sacred.

It's the phone call after a long day. The second chance for a struggling student. The faculty meeting no one wants to attend but still needs. The calm presence you maintain when everything around you is falling apart.

You lead anyway because students are still watching. Because teachers still need models of what's possible. Because the world doesn't need perfect educators—it needs present ones.

And because—somewhere in the future—someone will say, "That was the moment I knew I mattered," and they will be talking about you.

Ways to Enhance What Matters Most

If research shows that one adult can change a student's life, then the question is: How can we be more deliberate about being that one?

You don't need a new curriculum. You need to engage more deeply with what you already have.

Take attendance as a chance to notice, not just record. End class with a moment of reflection instead of rushing. Understand that quiet students aren't disengaged—they're observing and waiting to feel safe.

In staff meetings, improvement might mean pointing out the tension others avoid, revisiting the colleague who was dismissed, or speaking up for the student who's been overlooked. These aren't big acts. They're cultural shifts—and they spread.

Boosting your impact doesn't mean pushing yourself more. It means anchoring yourself more deeply.

Your presence disrupts the pattern. A warmth in a cold system. A steady pulse in a high-pressure environment. You may not be able to change the entire system — but you can make sure no one feels invisible while you're there.

Culture doesn't change with policies alone. It evolves through people—especially those who decide to lead, regardless.

MOSAIC IN ACTION

At a large urban high school, an instructional coach noticed that one veteran teacher, Mr. Liu, always lingered in the hallway after dismissal. Not because he had duties—but because he knew students didn't always rush home. One day, he saw a student crumple a college flyer into the trash. Without saying much, he walked over, picked it up, and handed it back with a quiet "You should still consider it." That simple act sparked a conversation, which led to a mentorship, culminating in a college application.

It wasn't flashy. It wasn't part of a program. It was simply presence.

Lead Anyway Reflection

- When have you stepped up even when it was inconvenient, unrecognized, or uncomfortable? What did it show about your character?
- What motivates you when your efforts don't show immediate results?
- Who guided you that way once—and how did it alter your story?
- What does it look like for you, in your specific role, to lead anyway this week?
- How do you want your students—or your team—to recall your presence?

> **TOOL TO TRY:**
> **Use the "Still a Good Person" Test**

When you're unsure about saying no, ask yourself: "If I decline this, am I still a good educator? A good teammate?" (Answer: Yes.) Boundaries respect your humanity, not your guilt.

> **TOOL TO TRY:**
> **Anchor Your Yes**

Before saying yes to something new, finish this sentence: "I'm saying yes because it aligns with _____." If you can't finish it with conviction, the yes may cost too much.

CHAPTER 11

From Compliance to Courage

The Student Who Said No

It wasn't disrespectful. It wasn't loud. However, it was bold.
During a writing prompt, a high school student quietly pushed his journal away. When the teacher asked why, he shrugged. "I'm tired of writing about things that don't matter to me."

There was a pause. Then came the instinct to redirect: "Well, this is part of the assignment." But something in the teacher shifted. Instead of pushing, she asked, "What would matter to you?"

"Courageous classrooms don't just manage behavior—they nurture bold, becoming minds."

That moment changed the whole classroom.

For years, education has equated compliance with success: sit still, follow directions, complete the task, and don't push back. We've trained generations to meet expectations—whether or not they make sense, feel fair, or reflect lived experiences.

But we are now teaching a generation that is not satisfied with silence.

They seek relevance. They want to be heard. And sometimes, they choose to say no.

Not out of rebellion—but out of awakening.

And that, if we allow it, can be the beginning of genuine learning.

Today's classrooms are influenced by generational changes. Many students—especially those in Gen Z and Gen Alpha—have grown up in a world full of information, witnessing injustice firsthand, and are comfortable discussing identity, mental health, and advocacy. They aren't afraid to question, take a pause, or challenge ideas.

Meanwhile, many of their educators—often from Gen X or Millennial cohorts—were raised in systems that rewarded compliance, masked emotion, and discouraged dissent.

This dissonance isn't a crisis; it's an invitation to evolve.

Not to abandon structure, but to lead with curiosity.

Not to loosen expectations, but to deepen relevance.

Not to control every moment, but to recognize that courage sometimes looks like quiet resistance—and learning often begins when someone dares to say, "This doesn't speak to me."

This is the invitation:

To teach beyond compliance.

To lead through discomfort.

And to create classrooms where courage is not punished but cultivated.

The Cost of Over-Compliance

Many of today's educators grew up in systems that valued silence and punished deviation. Compliance was seen as maturity, and conformity as discipline. Looking back, many of us weren't truly learning — we were just performing. We learned how to give the "right" answer, not how to ask better questions.

Over-compliance leads to students who can pass tests but don't question authority. It results in classrooms that are quiet but uncurious and teams that are agreeable but uninnovative. Over time, it fosters a culture where safety is found in invisibility rather than engagement.

For educators, this legacy persists. We stay quiet in staff meetings when something doesn't seem right. We hesitate to point out equity gaps out of fear of "disrupting unity." We follow pacing guides, even when they aren't in our students' best interest—not because we lack courage, but because compliance is deeply rooted in our professional identity.

Yet courage, not obedience, is the foundation of transformation. Education cannot grow until we start to value it, both in our students and ourselves.

Cultivating Brave Spaces

Courage in classrooms doesn't require chaos; it requires clarity. It encourages students to ask questions without fear and allows teachers to say, "This isn't working," without judgment. It creates space for administrators to say, "Let's try a new way," without needing to know the outcome in advance.

Creating brave spaces is not just about removing structure; it's about fostering integrity.

It involves listening when leadership is easier. It requires adapting when outdated rules hinder new realities. It entails naming discomfort and remaining with it long enough to understand it.

And most importantly, it means inviting people to bring their whole selves into the room—not just the parts that fit.

 MOSAIC IN ACTION

During a staff meeting on discipline procedures, Ms. Patel raised her hand—not to challenge leadership, but to ask, "Do these policies reflect who our students are now, or who they were ten years ago?" The room fell silent. She wasn't accusatory. She was clear. And that clarity sparked a follow-up conversation where staff reexamined assumptions they hadn't questioned in years. It wasn't defiance—it was emotional leadership. And it moved the work forward.

What the Research Shows

This chapter is based not only on lived experience but also on my doctoral research into identity fragmentation and emotional labor among Western educators working in international and culturally complex settings. One of the clearest findings was this: when identity expression is suppressed—whether in students or educators—engagement decreases, and burnout increases. Conversely, when classrooms become spaces where individuals feel recognized and encouraged to speak from their whole selves, transformation begins.

A 2022 study published in Educational Researcher similarly found that classrooms emphasizing psychological safety, open dialogue, and identity expression had higher student engagement, especially among students who have been historically marginalized in traditional schooling. These environments also encouraged more creative problem-solving, deeper academic risk-taking, and increased civic awareness.

In contrast, over-managed classrooms—where behavior was tightly controlled and expression was limited—had short-term gains but led to long-term disengagement, especially in middle and high school settings.

The data clearly shows: courage is not a distraction from learning. It is the foundation of lasting learning.

Leadership That Models Courage

Students will be as courageous as their teachers are honest. Teams will innovate to the extent that leaders allow vulnerability. And schools will heal to the degree that someone dares to speak the truth out loud.

You can teach standards while fostering courage. You can meet objectives while still encouraging questioning. You can follow policy while questioning the aspects that don't make sense for your students.

This isn't about defiance; it's about alignment. Leading from the truth rather than tradition, choosing presence over perfection, and encouraging others to do the same.

Because compliance might keep the room quiet, but courage? Courage changes everything.

LEAD ANYWAY

Enhancing Learning Through Courage

If the research is clear on anything, it is this: the most effective classrooms are not the quietest—they are the bravest. When students are invited to bring their full selves into the learning environment, engagement deepens, creativity expands, and the room becomes a living space for growth. Yet courage does not emerge from content alone. It must be cultivated—through intentional practices that encourage expression, honor vulnerability, and reframe the very nature of learning.

One of the most effective ways educators can improve the learning environment is by making space for identity expression. This isn't about reserving time for occasional cultural activities or poster projects; it's about integrating identity-affirming practices into the everyday routine of the classroom. When students are encouraged to bring their language, stories, families, and perspectives into their work, they stop trying to fit in and begin showing up authentically.

Courageous classrooms start with emotionally open leadership. When teachers show how to handle uncertainty, admit when something is unclear, or share the personal "why" behind their work, students see that authenticity is a strength, not a liability. Emotional transparency breaks down the myth of perfection and fosters an environment where questions are not only welcomed but are crucial.

This extends to how we handle discipline and accountability. Over-managed classrooms might achieve short-term compliance, but they often undermine the very trust that enables long-term growth. When educators move from control to dialogue—substituting punitive measures with restorative conversations—they uphold dignity while still maintaining expectations. These moments are not signs of weakness; they are times when leadership embraces humanity.

But courage without structure isn't leadership—it's confusion. Some classrooms encourage student voice without establishing shared agreements or boundaries, and the result isn't empowerment but a loss of control. When we invite critique without community, or expression without expectations, we risk creating spaces that feel unpredictable and unsafe—not just for teachers, but for students as well.

In a kindergarten classroom, this might look like encouraging students to "lead their own learning" without demonstrating how to share space, take turns, or ask thoughtful questions. The result? Disrupted routines, overwhelmed peers, and a teacher constantly firefighting instead of guiding.

In middle school, educators might encourage students to "be themselves" or "speak their truth" without providing guidance on emotional regulation or group norms. Without structure, this can often lead to sarcasm, peer conflict, or performative disruptions—because students are still learning how to express emotions in socially appropriate ways.

In a high school environment, a well-meaning effort to encourage open dialogue about injustice can backfire when students start using unfiltered language, which may offend peers or reinforce stereotypes—because no shared norms were set beforehand.

In college classrooms, professors may host "open forums" for student opinions but often do not intervene when misinformation, tone-policing, or microaggressions occur. The silence doesn't feel like freedom—it feels like abandonment.

Courage requires containment, not control. Students flourish when their bravery is backed by clear boundaries, collaboratively developed agreements, and adults who are both emotionally engaged and structurally reliable.

Enhancement also involves encouraging students to critique—not just texts, but systems. When a classroom motivates students to ask, "Why is it this way?" and "Whose voice is missing?" they are not acting rebelliously; they are being prepared. Prepared to challenge inequality. Prepared to notice subtle differences. Prepared to lead. This kind of critical inquiry strengthens both academic skills and civic awareness, making sure that students leave not only knowledgeable but also empowered.

It is just as important to include courageous pauses—moments during the instructional day when students can reflect, process, and speak freely. In a fast-paced school system, silence might seem like lost time. However, reflection is not a detour; it is the core of meaning-making. Whether through journaling, class discussions, or simple breathwork, giving students permission to slow down often speeds up their growth in meaningful ways.

And finally, we must teach students that mistakes are not signs of failure; they are proof of learning in progress. When we value the process over the final result and celebrate persistence instead of only achievement, we change the culture from fear to resilience. Students no longer shy away from challenges; they step up to meet them.

Courage, then, is not just a soft skill or a side project. It is the foundation where deep learning takes root. It shows up in how we structure our lessons, how we speak to students, and how we respond when things go wrong. It exists in the risks we take to tell the truth, the grace we show when others try, and the daily choice to lead with presence rather than perfection.

Ultimately, courage not only improves learning but also changes it.

The Courage to Slow Down

One of the most underestimated types of courage in education is the courage to slow down.

In an environment controlled by curriculum maps, pacing guides, and high-stakes assessments, slowing down can feel like failure. Teachers are aware of the benchmarks. They see the upcoming test dates. They feel the pressure to "cover everything." And yet—deep learning rarely occurs on a tightrope.

Slowing down does not mean abandoning academic rigor. It means recognizing that depth is not the enemy of progress. It's the foundation of it. When educators pause for reflection, dialogue, emotional check-ins, or unexpected learning moments, they are not "losing time"—they are investing it in making meaning.

The challenge is real: curriculum timelines rarely bend. But educators can still insert micro-pauses—15-minute reflective activities, an unplanned day for regrouping after a heavy unit, or a moment to recalibrate when the emotional tone in the room shifts. These choices require courage, not because they are radical, but because they run counter to a system fixated on pace rather than presence.

The Mosaic Intelligence Method™ supports this tension.

Emotional integrity encourages us to recognize what students are bearing, not just academically but emotionally.

Cultural flexibility lets us adapt to the situation in front of us, not just stick to the plan we have.

Identity agility allows us to lead in new ways—adapting when something more essential is required, without viewing it as a sign of weakness.

The truth is, learning without reflection is just information, not true transformation.

And courageous teaching isn't about how much we cover—It's about what actually takes hold.

Five Ways to Build Reflection into a Fast-Paced Week

Small Shifts. Big Impact.

1. One-Minute Check-In

Start or end class with a single reflective question:

"What's something that surprised you today?"

"What's one word for how you're showing up right now?"

Use index cards, a sticky note, or verbal responses. The goal is not grading—it's presence.

2. Journal Pause (Even for 3–5 Minutes)

Choose one day a week to pause instruction for reflective writing. Prompts like "What's something you've learned that matters to you?"

or "Where did you feel stuck this week?" invite depth with minimal disruption.

3. Emotional Debrief Moments

After a difficult discussion, test, or group activity, take 2–3 minutes to process the experience:

"What did we notice?"

"What emotions came up?"

Normalize emotional insight as part of academic growth.

4. Reclaim a Lesson Ending

Set aside the last 5 minutes of class once a week for "Slow Down Synthesis." Instead of rushing to the bell, ask students to share what stood out, what they still wonder about, or how it connects to their life. Write their responses on the board, a shared document, or a community journal.

5. Midweek Reset Ritual

Create a simple weekly routine for recalibration—stretching, breathwork, quiet drawing, or partner reflection. Just five minutes in the middle of the week sends a clear message to students (and yourself): we are more than what we produce.

Lead Anyway Reflection

- Where in your classroom, department, or leadership do you associate silence with success?
- What systems or expectations are you adhering to that no longer serve your students or uphold your integrity?
- How can you foster courageous dialogue in environments where compliance is the norm?
- When was the last time you asked for honest feedback and really listened?
- What's one way you can show more courage in your leadership this week, even if the outcome is uncertain?

TOOL TO TRY:
Release the Performance Script

When you catch yourself overexplaining or overdoing, pause and ask: "Am I performing for approval—or teaching from presence?" Superteachers aren't sustainable. Grounded ones are.

TOOL TO TRY:
Pick One Thing to Drop

This week, pick one small thing to let go of—not because of failure, but as a strategy. Say it aloud: "I'm releasing this to preserve my energy for what matters more."

CHAPTER 12

Centering Student Voice Without Losing Your Own

The Day They Took Over

It started as a lesson on media bias. Mr. Shah opened the floor for student input, expecting insightful examples or commentary related to the day's objectives. Instead, a student raised their hand and asked, "Can we talk about how the school itself chooses what voices to highlight and which ones it silences?"

What began as a discussion turned into disruption—but not the kind the teacher feared. Students spoke openly about inconsistent discipline, which student groups received funding, and how some identities were more closely monitored than others.

"Your voice matters, too. Centering students is not the same as erasing yourself."

Mr. Shah didn't interrupt. He let them speak. He held the space. But afterward, he felt rattled, even dismissed.

Later that evening, he wondered if he had lost control. But the class had done what he always said he wanted: they engaged critically. They questioned norms. They showed leadership. What he hadn't expected was how much it would challenge him, too.

DR. KARISSA THOMAS

The Risk and Reward of Amplifying Student Voice

We often claim we value student voice. We publish the quotes. We hang posters. We run surveys. But when students truly speak—when their truths challenge the systems we've become used to—it can feel uncomfortable, even destabilizing.

It's simple to amplify student voice when it aligns with our views. It becomes more difficult when it challenges our curriculum, questions our authority, or uncovers blind spots we haven't addressed yet.

Supporting student voice isn't a one-time act; it's an ongoing practice. It requires humility, patience, and awareness. It means remaining emotionally grounded when what we hear stings and holding back the instinct to defend when we're asked to listen.

You Still Belong in the Room

One common myth about student-centered leadership is that teachers must step back completely. However, prioritizing student voice doesn't mean you have to silence your own. Students don't want us to disappear—they need us to be emotionally present and culturally grounded.

In my doctoral research on Western educators in international schools, a recurring theme surfaced: when teachers feel invisible or disconnected from their own identities, they find it difficult to create space for student expression. The internal conflict between professional expectations and personal authenticity leaves little emotional capacity to handle critique.

Educators who feel overlooked are less likely to empower others.

Leading with presence involves recognizing your own value while allowing others to grow. When students observe us modeling emotional regulation, boundary-setting, and dialogue under pressure, they learn that leadership isn't about dominance. It's about discernment.

Student Voice Is Not the Same as Student Agreement

Too often, we mistake student voice for student conformity. If students agree, we praise their involvement. If they disagree—particularly when it challenges comfort—we categorize it as defiance.

But true voice is independent of agreement. It reflects trust, not submission. It means students feel safe enough to share what's real for them—even when it complicates our lesson plan.

You don't need to be liked to be effective. You just need to be present, trustworthy, and open.

What the Research Says

A 2023 report from the Stanford Center for Opportunity Policy in Education found that schools with high levels of genuine student voice—characterized by co-created norms, student advisory roles, and responsive classroom structures—experienced significantly higher student engagement, increased academic risk-taking, and better civic readiness. Students, especially from historically marginalized groups, demonstrated more resilience and a stronger sense of agency when their voices were met with consistent adult follow-through.

However, the same report noted that when student voice was tokenized—treated as a checkbox without real influence—disillusionment occurred. Especially for students of color and LGBTQ+ students, being asked for input and then ignored caused deeper disengagement than if they hadn't been asked at all.

Student voice without adult follow-through remains just performance. However, student voice combined with emotionally intelligent leadership leads to transformation.

Holding Space Without Losing Center

To center student voice without losing your own requires inner clarity. It involves knowing who you are, what you value, and how you plan to show up—even when conversations become difficult. This isn't about overpowering students, nor is it about stepping aside. It's about grounding yourself so others feel safe to step forward.

This is where the **Mosaic Intelligence Method™** proves vital.

Emotional integrity keeps you centered when feedback hurts or students challenge your decisions.

Cultural flexibility helps you stay curious about differences instead of becoming defensive.

Identity agility allows you to grow alongside your students—broadening your understanding without losing your core.

You don't have to choose between student empowerment and teacher authority.

In fact, the most transformative classrooms are led by adults who are both steady and spacious—anchored in their values while being open to student voice. These educators don't confuse stillness with silence or boundaries with control. They lead from wholeness while encouraging dialogue, difference, and discovery.

The goal isn't to control the conversation.

The goal is to shape it with care, hold it with presence, and stay grounded enough to make room for growth—on all sides.

Student Voice in a Rigid System

Dr. Elaine Kim, a sociology professor at a mid-sized university, wanted to prioritize student perspectives—but her syllabus was constrained by departmental goals and accreditation requirements. So she organized a "student-led dialogue" week at midterm. Students selected readings, developed questions, and led peer discussions. The structure remained—the focus shifted. Students began to see themselves as scholars, not just as recipients of instruction. Dr. Kim didn't abandon the system—she adapted it, just enough to create space for student voice.

MOSAIC IN ACTION

Small Moments of Emotional Integrity and Identity Agility

When a student challenged Ms. Rivera's grading policy during a class discussion, her first instinct was to explain and defend. But instead, she paused and asked, "Tell me more—what about it feels unfair to you?" The student hesitated and then shared how certain assignments disproportionately impacted students who worked after school. Ms. Rivera didn't immediately change the policy. Instead, she listened, took it to her department, and came back the next week with an adjusted rubric, thanking the student for raising the concern. That moment had a ripple effect—across the class and the school culture.

Her Mosaic Intelligence in action:

Emotional integrity: She maintained her composure by resisting defensiveness and staying true to her values.

Cultural flexibility: She thought about how her policy affects students with different responsibilities.

Identity agility: She adapted her role—not as a rule enforcer, but as a responsive leader.

Small adjustments build big trust. That's how leadership becomes empowering.

Lead Anyway Reflection

- When was the last time you sincerely sought student feedback—and did you let it change you?
- How are you protecting your authority at the cost of student voice?
- How do you remain rooted in your values when others push back?
- Where might you be confusing discomfort with disrespect?
- What would it look like to lead from a stance of co-creation instead of control?

TOOL TO TRY:
Rotate the Mic

Choose one class activity this week where students take the lead—from guiding discussions to curating examples. Show them their voice matters by giving them the structure to practice it.

TOOL TO TRY:
Say What You Need, Too

In moments of classroom tension, try: "Your voice matters. And so does mine." Co-regulation works both ways. You don't have to disappear to create space for others.

CHAPTER 13

What the Data Doesn't Show

The Perfect Report Card, The Silent Crisis

When Maya's report card arrived, it showed straight A's. Her attendance was flawless, and her behavior record was impeccable. Her teachers described her as "polite," "independent," and "well-organized." On paper, she was excelling.

But what the data didn't show was the panic attacks before school, the lunch periods she spent hiding in the bathroom, scrolling just to feel numb, and the fact that she hadn't spoken in class in three weeks—not because she didn't know the answers, but because she felt invisible in every conversation.

"Not everything that transforms is measurable—but it still matters."

Her success story was founded on silence.

Educators sensed something was wrong, but nothing in the system raised concern. No referrals. No absences. No missing work. Her nervous system was unsettled, but the spreadsheet marked her as "on track."

This illustrates the danger of confusing metrics with meaning. What the data doesn't reveal is often what truly matters.

The Limits of the Score Sheet

Education thrives on numbers. We track them, report them, and develop policies based on them. But no score reveals whether a student feels safe. No dashboard shows who feels like an outsider. No spreadsheet captures the emotional toll of enduring a system designed for speed rather than connection.

We commend the students who follow quietly, but we often overlook those in silent survival mode.

Some students meet every deadline, not out of joy but because they fear being noticed. Others act out, not in rebellion but as a response to unseen trauma. Many disengage, not due to lack of ability, but because of a deeper message they've internalized: "This space is not for me."

Our systems react to what we see, but that doesn't always reflect the truth.

You Can't Quantify a Breakthrough

There's no checkbox for the student who finally made eye contact after months of withdrawal. No rubric score for the one who trusted you enough to whisper, "I need help." No graph that measures the shift from compliance to curiosity or from silence to self-expression.

Growth doesn't always appear as an upward trend. Sometimes, it's the quiet bravery of simply staying in the room.

We've created entire systems to measure learning—but few to understand it. That gap is where burnout, disconnection, and inequality grow.

What the Research Says

A 2022 report from the Learning Policy Institute finds that while data can reveal trends, it often does not capture the emotional, relational, and identity-based factors that drive student success. Schools with stronger relational cultures consistently perform better—even when their test scores are modest or their resources are limited.

The same study cautioned against "data dependency," pointing out that relying solely on metrics can result in superficial interventions—especially for students from historically marginalized communities. In other words: data is a flashlight, not a mirror.

My research confirmed this truth in cross-cultural, multilingual classrooms—where Western teachers worked in environments shaped by both cultural complexity and linguistic differences. In these settings, the formal curriculum often overlooked the emotional effort needed to connect across languages, norms, and unspoken values. Teachers recalled moments when student silence wasn't apathy—it was translation. When eye contact wasn't defiance—it was respect expressed differently. When discomfort wasn't disengagement—it was real-time identity negotiation.

These findings showed that what remains unseen in data is often what matters most in daily teaching and learning experiences. Emotional connection. Cultural misalignment. Language as both a barrier and a bridge.

In these global classrooms, success was seldom measured by test scores. Instead, it was about who felt seen, who felt safe to speak, and who could bring their whole self into the room—without needing to leave their language or culture at the door.

Teaching With a Broader Perspective

To lead with integrity, we must expand our view. The numbers are important—but so are what they hide. What stories are absent from this spreadsheet? Who stays quiet because they don't feel safe? What does success cost some students emotionally?

These are not "extra" questions. They are crucial ones.

Schools don't just shape minds — they shape identities. Ignoring the full human story means we're not truly educating; we're just performing.

But what happens when we can't communicate effectively? What if the student in front of us doesn't speak English—yet still needs to feel safe, known, and capable?

This is more than just a language challenge. It's a leadership challenge.

In many American classrooms today, students are juggling content, culture, and language all at once. Many of their teachers—well-meaning, skilled, and dedicated—still feel unprepared to close that gap. There may be no shared words, but shared humanity can still exist.

This is where the **Mosaic Intelligence Method™** becomes not only helpful but also essential.

Emotional integrity reminds us that presence surpasses words. A gentle tone, a patient pause, a small gesture of acknowledgment—these convey safety even when language falls short.

Cultural flexibility helps us suspend assumptions. It enables us to ask: What could this silence signify in their world—not just mine?

Identity agility allows us to lead with humility, admitting what we don't know and learning alongside our students without shame.

We address this not by speaking louder or oversimplifying, but by slowing down, listening more attentively, and remembering that language is just one way to communicate. Relationships are shaped through tone, gestures, rhythm, and repetition. They are built through the consistent act of trying.

Your Presence Is the Real Metric

Data has its role. But your presence, intuition, and insight are what truly influence outcomes. You notice what's left unsaid. You catch the sighs, the silence, the shift in energy. That's data too.

It might not appear in the report—but it's reflected in your leadership.

Your ability to read the room, pause before reacting, or follow up after a tough moment has more impact than any metric can show.

Especially when the words aren't there—your presence still remains.

Improving Practice Beyond the Metrics

Serving students well—especially those often overlooked—requires moving beyond just the numbers. Data can give a snapshot, but it can't tell the full story. Test scores indicate trends but don't reveal trauma, resilience, or the silent struggles behind performance.

Transformative teaching goes beyond measurement; it involves creating meaning.

That begins with different questions. Not "Who's failing?" but "What have we failed to see?" Not "What's the average?" but "Whose story is missing?"

We must also recognize the importance of observation. The teacher who notices a student's shrinking posture, or the administrator who pauses to defuse tension—these are data gatherers, too. They're reading bodies, not just benchmarks.

We should value storytelling as a form of evidence. The narratives students share—about identity, struggle, and self-worth—are educational tools. Creating space for them isn't a distraction; it's how equity becomes real.

The pressure to quantify everything is real. But metrics can become a shield—blocking us from the emotional labor that equity demands. We forget that education isn't just academic. It's human.

This is where the Mosaic Intelligence Method™ steps in. It reminds us that what matters most—emotional integrity, cultural flexibility, and identity agility—can't always be measured. But it can always be felt.

Using this broader perspective, we lead through alignment, not assumptions. From storytelling, not just standard practices.

Because behind every data point is a person. Behind every gap is a layered identity. And behind every student is someone waiting to be seen.

But in a system that increasingly prioritizes efficiency, even presence is now at risk of being automated. As AI becomes more accessible, a new level of invisibility threatens both students and staff—the replacement of genuine voice with artificial polish.

The Illusion of Productivity

AI, Authenticity, and the Human Cost

As AI tools become more accessible, a new challenge arises—one that traditional data seldom shows: the subtle decline of genuine engagement.

In classrooms, students now submit AI-generated essays that read smoothly but lack emotional depth or real-life experience. These assignments may meet the requirements, but they reveal very little about the person behind them. The writing is technically accurate—but emotionally empty. Expression is delegated. Voice is dulled.

And it's not just students. In schools across the country, some administrators now use AI to craft praise emails, send disciplinary notices, or respond to parent concerns. The messages are polished, with perfect grammar. But the human touch? Often missing.

On the surface, this might seem like efficiency.

But beneath that, it raises more concerning questions:

Who is actually present in the room? Whose voice are we hearing? What happens to growth, trust, or relational culture when communication is driven by algorithms?

This isn't a rejection of AI; it's a call to use it responsibly.

AI can assist with scaffolding, idea generation, feedback loops, and accessibility—but it cannot replace the emotional labor, voice, or presence that define real teaching and leadership.

When students rely on AI to avoid the discomfort of starting, revising, or reflecting, they rob themselves of the struggle—and miss the moment when real learning occurs. They choose convenience over voice, process over product.

When school leaders use AI to avoid difficult conversations or automate care, they sacrifice relationships for efficiency—and the impact is felt, even if it isn't acknowledged.

Authentic learning is messy, and so is leadership. Both need presence, not perfection.

We must teach students and demonstrate to staff that being fully human—in our writing, in our feedback, in our decisions—is not just an ethical stance. It is the foundation of trust, growth, and meaningful transformation.

> **TOOL TO TRY:**
> **Reclaiming Voice in an AI Age**

Helping Students Reflect on Integrity, Effort, and Identity in Their Work

Title: *"Was That My Voice?"*

Use: After an assignment, especially one involving writing or technology-supported work.

Steps:

1. **Private Reflection (3–5 min):**
    Ask students to answer in writing:
    "What part of this work came directly from *you*?"
    "What was hardest for you—and what did you learn from that part?"
    "If someone read this out loud, would they hear *you* in it?"
2. **Small Group Share (Optional):**
    In pairs or triads, students can (voluntarily) share one insight from their reflection and listen for patterns around struggle, voice, and growth.
3. **Whole Class Closing Prompt:**
    "What makes something feel like *your* work—not just work you completed?"

Purpose:

This tool is not about policing AI use—it's about helping students pause long enough to ask:

Is this mine? Did I grow through it? Did it reflect something true about me?

TOOL TO TRY:
Before You Send That AI-Generated Memo

Helping Leaders Use AI with Integrity, Presence, and Relational Awareness

Title: *"Should This Come From Me?"*

Use: Before sending messages—especially those involving praise, feedback, discipline, or policy decisions.

Ask Yourself These Three Questions:

1. **"Does this message require emotional presence?"**
   If the communication involves loss, discipline, celebration, or conflict—consider writing it yourself, even if it takes longer.
   AI can help draft policy. It shouldn't deliver care.
2. **"Am I hiding behind polish?"**
   Is AI smoothing out something I don't want to say myself? Am I outsourcing clarity or conflict resolution because it feels hard?
   If the AI version makes it easier to avoid discomfort, it may also avoid responsibility.
3. **"Will the person receiving this feel seen—or managed?"**
   Leadership isn't just about communication—it's about connection. If the message is relational in nature, it needs your tone, your story, and your fingerprints.
   Presence travels, even through text.

Reminder:

AI is a support tool, not a replacement. Efficiency without empathy might save time, but it erodes trust.

Leading with Mosaic Integrity in a Digital Age

The future of education isn't just about access to technology—it's about developing emotional literacy in digital spaces. AI will influence how we write, research, and communicate. However, it should never replace the essential work of reflection, building relationships, and being truly present.

The Mosaic Intelligence Method™ doesn't reject innovation. It simply asks:

Are we still showing up as ourselves?
Are we still leading with care?
Are we still making space for the human story beneath the surface?

Because in the age of automation, the most powerful thing we can offer is genuine presence.

MOSAIC IN ACTION

A Moment of Data-Defying Presence

Mr. Taylor noticed that Isaiah—a straight-A student—had started submitting his work earlier than usual. His essays were flawless. His participation was consistent. But his eyes were dull. His humor was gone.

Instead of praising the improvement, Mr. Taylor asked him to stay after class.

They sat silently for a minute.

"You doing okay?" Mr. Taylor asked quietly.

Isaiah shrugged. "I'm tired. Like… deep tired."

That simple exchange triggered a quiet unraveling. Isaiah opened up about stress at home, the pressure to perform, and the exhaustion of keeping it all together. Mr. Taylor referred him for support—and more importantly, helped him scale back his workload in a way that maintained both his dignity and his mental health.

This was **Mosaic Intelligence Method** in action:

Emotional integrity: Mr. Taylor trusted his instincts and prioritized presence over performance.

Cultural flexibility: He didn't link achievement to wellness—or silence to stability.

Identity agility: He transitioned from evaluator to advocate, adapting his role instantly to address Isaiah's human needs.

Not all metrics reveal the truth.

Sometimes, leadership involves noticing what the report doesn't mention—and having the courage to respond regardless.

Lead Anyway Reflection

- What have you discovered about your students that no test score could show?
- Where are you depending on data for decisions that need more careful judgment?
- How can you make room for student stories—not just grades—to influence your teaching?
- What would change if your school prioritized trust and emotional safety as much as attendance and test results?
- How do you want your leadership to be remembered—by the data you tracked or by the lives you touched?

> **TOOL TO TRY:**
> **Model Calm Power**

When disrespect arises, pause before responding. Speak with steady clarity: "Let's reset—this space deserves better from both of us." It communicates strength without escalating the situation.

> **TOOL TO TRY:**
> **Clarify the Boundary, Not Just the Behavior**

Instead of saying, "Don't talk to me like that," try: "This is a space where we speak with respect. I'm holding that line—for both of us." Boundaries work best when rooted in values.

CHAPTER 14

Wholeness as a Leadership Strategy

The Educator Who Refused to Break in Half

Ms. Collier was known for her excellence. Her classroom was a model site. Her students thrived. But no one knew that every night, she cried in her car before going home, as she managed aging parents, her own anxiety, and a workload that kept stretching beyond what was reasonable.

"You don't have to break to belong. You can lead from a place that's full, not fractured."

She had mastered professionalism but felt broken inside. She maintained a "teacher self" and a "real self," and the distance between them was widening. It wasn't until she fell seriously ill—that she understood: survival is not leadership. Performance is not presence. And excellence that costs you your wholeness is not sustainable.

Her return to the classroom wasn't about reinventing herself; it was about integration. She started recognizing her limits. She allowed herself to be seen. She didn't stop striving—but she stopped dividing.

And everything changed.

We Were Never Meant to Lead in Pieces

Education often teaches us to compartmentalize, to smile through grief, to "stay strong" during a personal crisis, and to keep our real stories outside the school walls. We learn to lead in fragments, and then we wonder why we feel so empty.

Wholeness isn't about perfection. It's about alignment. It involves bringing your entire self into your work—your joy, your fatigue, your wisdom, your questions. It means leading in a way that doesn't sacrifice your own needs for others'.

You can't promote wellness while pushing yourself toward burnout. You can't preach authenticity while concealing your true self. You can't expect students or staff to show up fully if you're only revealing a small part of yourself.

The true challenge is integration.

Leadership That Breathes

Wholeness as a leadership strategy doesn't mean oversharing. It doesn't mean turning classrooms into therapy sessions or staff meetings into confessionals. It involves creating a culture where human experience isn't rejected—it's embraced.

It means slowing down while everyone else speeds up. It involves creating systems that mirror humanity rather than just adherence. It signifies making decisions that honor both your role and your rhythm.

When you lead from wholeness, your presence calms the room. You become a thermostat, not just a thermometer. You regulate—not because you're unaffected— but because you've made peace with your own pace.

What the Research Says

A 2022 report by the Carnegie Foundation for the Advancement of Teaching found that emotionally attuned school leaders—those who engage in regular self-reflection and maintain sustainable boundaries—have significantly better teacher retention, fewer workplace conflicts, and higher student trust ratings.

The same study emphasized that "emotional presence is a core condition for instructional excellence," especially in communities affected by trauma. In short, wholeness isn't optional—it's essential.

My own research confirms this, especially in cross-cultural and multilingual learning settings. Educators working across language differences and complex identities often bear an invisible emotional burden—translating not only content but also expectations, norms, and their own selves. Many reported feeling fragmented: expected to demonstrate strength while silently grappling with cultural dissonance or systemic invisibility.

This fragmentation didn't come from a lack of skill—but from a lack of space to appear whole.

Teachers and leaders who had space to align their values, emotions, and identities led with greater clarity and care. And when that alignment was supported institutionally — not just personally — they didn't just stay in the profession. They grew within it.

Wholeness, then, is not a luxury or a bonus.

It is the foundation of sustainable, human-centered leadership.

Integration Over Imitation

We don't need more leaders who imitate authority. We need leaders who demonstrate alignment, who bring their whole selves—not just their job titles—into the room, who know how to set standards without losing self-compassion, who tell the truth when they're exhausted, who take rest seriously, and who speak up when the system forgets its soul.

When you lead this way, you empower others to follow suit. You uphold dignity without insisting on perfection. And you remind everyone watching—including yourself—that wholeness is not a luxury but the foundation.

Enhancing Leadership Through Wholeness

The most effective leadership starts with oneself, not strategy. The research confirms what many educators have long sensed—it explicitly states it: emotional attunement is not merely a soft skill. It serves as the foundation of trust, stability, and transformation in schools; that attunement must begin internally.

To cultivate leadership from a place of wholeness is to shift away from performance and toward integration. This involves no longer compartmentalizing who you are just to appear in control. It means aligning your inner world with your outer leadership—so that the person who greets students in the morning, leads meetings in the afternoon, and reflects on the day privately is the same person. Not perfect, but present. Not invulnerable, but integrated.

This kind of leadership fosters safety for others. When a principal prioritizes rest, they challenge the usual burnout culture. When a department head openly states their limits without shame, they set boundaries that others can follow. When a leader openly discusses the toll of leadership—and still chooses to lead—they make courage infectious.

Enhancing wholeness in practice also means creating school environments that support emotional sustainability, not just academic outcomes. Staff need spaces to process—not just to plan. They need leaders who ask, "How are you holding up?" and genuinely mean it. They require systems that honor humanity without sacrificing excellence. These are not opposing forces. In fact, excellence becomes more attainable when people are emotionally well.

True enhancement isn't about adding more to your plate. It's about removing the performance drains that deplete your energy and reclaiming practices that restore it. Self-reflection, boundary setting, purposeful pauses—these aren't acts of resistance; they are acts of leadership. The clearer you are with yourself, the clearer your impact becomes.

This also challenges the myth that leadership requires imitation. We don't need copies of authority figures from the past. We need educators who lead with presence, not posturing; who can raise the bar without draining their soul; who can hold others accountable while showing themselves compassion. That is the leadership students notice. That is the leadership teams trust. And that is the leadership that endures.

LEAD ANYWAY

This is the core of the Mosaic Intelligence Method™: leading with emotional integrity, grounded in self-awareness; practicing cultural adaptability, rooted in collective care; and demonstrating identity agility, shaped by authentic alignment. When leaders embody these qualities, they do more than just perform well—they lead as whole persons. In doing so, they inspire others to do the same.

When wholeness is seen not as a reward for surviving, but as a foundation for leading, the culture begins to change. In that change, schools become more than just places of learning; they transform into ecosystems of belonging, care, and resilience.

Because at the end of the day, it is not charisma that sustains a leader; it is congruence. When you lead from that place, everyone around you feels the difference.

MOSAIC IN ACTION

Rest as Resistance, Wholeness as Leadership

After a particularly tough quarter, Ms. Collier made an unexpected choice—she used her last personal day not for errands or grading catch-up, but to sit in the park with her journal. That afternoon, she realized her rest wasn't a retreat—it was a reset. When she came back, she didn't apologize for the break. She openly shared with her team about the pressure she had been under and the boundaries she was reestablishing. Her honesty changed the atmosphere. Staff meetings became less performative. A few coworkers took mental health days without feeling guilty. One even started arriving on time instead of two hours early "just to get ahead." Her quiet act of wholeness sparked a ripple of cultural change.

Her Mosaic Intelligence in action

> **Emotional Integrity:** She acknowledged the toll her role had taken and allowed herself to take a pause.

Cultural Flexibility: She redefined what "dedication" meant in her context, changing norms.

Identity Agility: She aligned her internal needs with her external leadership without apology.

Opportunity: Wholeness isn't indulgent; it's instructive.

Lead Anyway Reflection

- Where in your leadership have you been inconsistent, and what is that costing you?
- What parts of your story have you been hiding because you're worried they don't "belong" in professional spaces?
- How can you begin to lead from a place of integration—not just through role performance?
- What would shift in your classroom or school if wholeness—not exhaustion—became the main goal?
- How would your presence change if you stopped dividing and started showing up as your true self?

TOOL TO TRY:
Define Your Leadership Baseline

Before the week starts, ask yourself: "What do I want my presence to communicate?" Write down one core value and one boundary you'll protect. Revisit it midweek to stay aligned—not just efficient.

**TOOL TO TRY:
Regulate, Then Respond**

When tension rises, pause before reacting. Breathe. Ask: "What does this moment actually need from me?" Then lead from presence, not pressure.

CHAPTER 15

Lead Anyway – The Invitation to Evolve

A System Can't Save Us—But We Can Change It

There will always be new initiatives, new acronyms, new rubrics, and new tools. Education is never lacking in change. However, we often confuse change with transformation.

Transformation doesn't begin with data dashboards or strategic plans. It starts with people—fully recognized, emotionally engaged, working within systems that truly honor their effort and the brilliance of their students.

"This is not a guidebook. It's a mirror. And you get to decide how you show up in it."

If the past few years have taught us anything, it's this: no technology, policy, or framework can replace the significance of being guided, taught, or mentored by someone who is fully human.

The future of education isn't about being faster; it's about being deeper. It's not about being more efficient; it's about being more connected. It's not about being more competitive; it's about being more compassionate.

We Are the System Now

There comes a moment when every educator realizes that no one is coming to fix it. Not the district. Not the department. Not the task force. That's not a moment of despair; it's a moment of awakening.

Because once we stop waiting for the system to change from the top down, we can start reshaping it from the inside out. In every classroom where a teacher slows down to listen, in every staff meeting where a leader speaks honestly, and in every office hour where a student feels recognized.

We are not just participants in the system; we are the culture itself. Culture changes when people change.

Leadership Is the Daily Choice to Stay Human

The work ahead won't be easy. Leading with emotional integrity, cultural awareness, and clarity about identity is not performative—it's disruptive. It means saying, "This doesn't work anymore," when others want to stay silent. It means protecting people, not just policies. It means asking tough questions, setting clear boundaries, and returning to the room—again and again—with your heart intact.

That type of leadership not only improves classrooms but also shapes better futures.

Whether you are a teacher, principal, assistant principal, counselor, or professor, you are shaping more than lesson plans. You are shaping people. The most powerful thing you can demonstrate is not perfection, control, or charisma.

It's about wholeness.

 MOSAIC IN ACTION

The Assistant Principal Who Modeled Permission

When Mr. Lewis began his new role as assistant principal, he inherited a team worn out by turnover, testing demands, and a culture of compliance. Instead of launching a full-scale overhaul, he started by holding weekly five-minute hallway check-ins. No forms. No metrics. Just being present.

He told the staff: "If you need to cry, you can cry. If you're angry, I'll listen. If you need silence, I'll stand with you."

By the end of the semester, staff attendance increased. Students reported feeling more emotionally supported. Not because a policy changed—but because the adults felt safer being themselves again.

His Mosaic Intelligence in action:

Emotional integrity: He accepts real feelings without fear.

Cultural flexibility: He acknowledged diverse emotional needs among staff.

Identity agility: He led without pretending to have it all together.

This kind of leadership encourages growth without requiring perfection.

What We Leave Behind

Years from now, students won't remember which platform you used, what grading policy you enforced, or how closely your objectives matched the latest framework. They will remember how they felt in your presence.

Did they feel safe?
Did they feel smart?
Did they feel like they mattered?
Your legacy isn't just a program; it's the emotional mark you leave behind.

The Work Isn't Finished—But You Are Ready

You don't need permission, a new title, or everything to be perfect before you start. What you already have—clarity, courage, and a belief that something better is possible—is enough.

The future of education is not just a new system; it's a new way of being inside it—a more human approach.

This is where the Mosaic Intelligence Method™ will guide us forward—not as a rigid solution, but as a compass for growth. It reminds us that wholeness is not a departure from leadership; it is the bravest form of it. Emotional integrity, cultural flexibility, and identity agility are not optional; they are vital.

And you are already part of that future. Every time you choose presence over pressure, people over policy, and wholeness over performance, you lead us forward.

Take a breath, stand tall, and lead regardless.

What If I Don't Have That Kind of Power?

Some educators might read this and think, "That's easy for someone else to say. I don't have a platform. I don't make the decisions. I'm just trying to get through the week without breaking."

That response isn't resistance.

It's honesty. And it deserves respect.

Because for many teachers, staff, and adjunct faculty—especially those from underrepresented backgrounds—the system has never been safe, fair, or sustainable. It rewards exhaustion. It silences critique. It calls innovation "noncompliance."

So no, a system can't save us.

But we can still lead anyway.

Leading still means acknowledging what's broken. It means choosing not to become it. It involves leading with presence, care, and courage—even in the smallest moments. Even when policies stay the same. Even when no one's watching.

Sometimes that leadership involves challenging a bias in a meeting.

Sometimes it's mentoring a colleague, advocating for a student, or setting clear boundaries. And sometimes—it's simply choosing to stay whole in a culture that encourages fragmentation.
You might not be able to change the system overnight.
But you can challenge what it expects from you.
That's where real change starts.

The Mosaic Internal Lesson Plan

Where the Lesson Is Going — and Where You Are Today

In a system that often demands constant performance, the most radical thing a teacher can do is pause long enough to notice how they're arriving to the day. This isn't about perfection—it's about presence, and making space for both the plan and the person who will carry it out. A lesson is never just its content; it's also the living, breathing human who delivers it. When we honor both, we make space for deeper learning and sustainable leadership.

Purpose:

Every lesson carries two stories: the planned path of learning and the lived presence of the teacher. Both shape the student experience. The Mosaic Internal Lesson Plan helps you honor both—recognizing that you don't have to show up perfect to show up powerfully. It is designed for personal grounding, peer collaboration, and leadership conversations that support growth without judgment.

---

1. Begin with the Teacher

Before thinking about the day's objectives, pause and notice: *Where am I arriving from?* This might be a word, an image, or a sentence. No scoring, no self-correction—just acknowledgment.

---

2. **Name the Focus of the Lesson**
In one or two sentences, describe where you want this lesson to lead. Not just the standard or objective, but the *impact*. What do you hope students feel, understand, or try differently by the end?

3. **Map the Experience**
Sketch the flow in simple terms: the opening that invites them in, the core activity that deepens the work, and the closing moment that lets the learning settle.

4. **Weave in the Mosaic Intelligence Method™**
Ask yourself:

- *Emotional Integrity:* How will I model honesty about challenges and successes?
- *Cultural Flexibility:* How will I make space for perspectives beyond my own?
- *Identity Agility:* Where might I step back so students can lead the thinking?

5. **Close with Reflection**
After the lesson, take a breath before moving on. Ask: *What stayed with me? What stayed with them?* Identify one small thing worth carrying forward and, if needed, one thing you'd release.

Leadership Use:
In observation or mentoring, this plan becomes a bridge for dialogue. Instead of asking "Did the teacher follow the plan?" it invites "What did the plan reveal about the day?"—turning observation into an act of partnership.

The Mosaic Internal Lesson Plan isn't just a task to complete or a form to fill out — it's a reminder that teaching and leading are ongoing, living processes. Some days, the plan will match your energy perfectly. Other days, it might feel like you're navigating through fog. Both experiences are a natural part of the work. What matters most is staying connected to your purpose, your people, and yourself. The reflection questions that follow are meant to help you maintain that connection beyond today's lesson and throughout your leadership journey.

Lead Anyway Reflection

- What kind of future are you helping create in your classroom or school—and is it aligned with your values?
- Where are you waiting for permission that isn't needed anymore?
- What would it involve to shift your leadership from compliance-driven to culture-influencing?
- How do you want your students, colleagues, or institution to remember your leadership—years after you've left?
- What small act of courage can you take this week that reflects the kind of future humanity needs through education?

TOOL TO TRY:
Create a 5-Minute Pause Ritual

Choose one part of your day—before class, after lunch, or before heading home—and take five quiet minutes. Not to plan. Not to perform. Just to breathe and reset.

DR. KARISSA THOMAS

TOOL TO TRY:
Track What Renews You

For one week, write down the moments that gave you energy—not drained it. Patterns will come to light. Let them guide you in protecting your energy moving forward.

Lead Anyway Tools: Practical Moves for the Mosaic Classroom

A Practical Companion to the Mosaic Intelligence Method™

Teaching through the fog doesn't just require insight—it requires action. And sometimes, what educators need most are tools they can actually use—tools that hold up when the classroom feels heavy, when the connection is fading, or when their own energy is running low.

This section acts as a bridge between theory and practice. It's crafted for real educators working in real schools, engaging in genuine emotional labor—those who believe in reflection but also need something to grasp onto when the day calls for clarity, not complexity. These moments emphasize presence over perfection, where leadership is judged not by control, but by connection.

"These aren't scripts—they're soul-level invitations to lead with humanity."

The following tools align with the Mosaic Intelligence Method™ and are organized around its three core capacities: **Emotional Integrity, Cultural Flexibility,** and **Identity Agility**. You don't need to use all of them. You're not asked to do more—you're invited to select what resonates. Adjust what feels too rigid. Trust your professional instinct. These aren't strict rules—they're invitations.

Emotional Integrity Tools

Lead with emotional truth, not performance.

We're often told to "show up strong"—but true strength in leadership starts with emotional honesty. Emotional integrity isn't about breaking down in front of your students or colleagues; it's about refusing to hide your inner experience in the name of professionalism. It's the courage to be present when perfection seems out of reach.

When you lead with emotional honesty, you foster a culture of safety—for yourself and those around you. These resources help you reset your nervous system, deepen self-awareness, and realign your emotions, especially on days when showing up feels the toughest.

1. The 1-Minute Reset (for you or your team)

Before a lesson or meeting, pause and ask yourself:
- What emotion am I bringing into this space?
- What's one thing I need to let go of to be more present?
- What would make this interaction feel more human?

Use it privately or invite your team to join. It's not a ritual for optics—it's a reset for clarity.

2. Feelings Forecast for Classrooms

At the start of class, invite a check-in (spoken or silent):
- I'm here and ready.
- I'm here but distracted.
- I'm here but struggling.

No explanations required—just awareness. Let this quiet data inform your pacing, tone, and approach for the day.

3. Emotional Anchor Phrases

When emotions run high or disconnection settles in, use phrases like:
- "Let's pause for a moment before we move forward."
- "I'm noticing some heaviness—what would help this space feel safer right now?"
- "You don't have to have it together. Let's figure it out together."

These aren't magic words. But they model what it looks like to lead with presence over pressure.

Cultural Flexibility Tools

Respond to complexity with curiosity, not control.

Culture enters every room long before curriculum does. Students bring their whole selves—language, tradition, trauma, resistance, brilliance—into our classrooms each day. Cultural flexibility isn't about having all the answers. It's about choosing curiosity over control, especially when differences emerge in unexpected ways.

These tools help you question your assumptions, design inclusively, and create environments that recognize the full identity spectrum of your students. True belonging doesn't come from being accepted into a rigid system—it comes from being seen for who you truly are.

4. Student Story Inventory (Beyond the Data)

Once per semester, offer students these reflective prompts:
- What's something about your background that influences how you learn?
- What do people often misunderstand about you in school?
- What kind of support actually helps you (even if others don't realize it)?

You're not looking for essays. You're looking for insight that shapes your leadership.

5. Classroom Culture Scan

Take 10 quiet minutes and reflect on the following:
- Whose stories, languages, or perspectives are missing from my curriculum?
- What norms in this room might unintentionally exclude or silence certain identities?
- What's one small change I can make to center inclusion more intentionally this month?

What you notice—and what you change—will shape more than content. It shapes belonging.

6. The Behavior Reframe Practice

Before reacting to behavior that feels disruptive, pause and ask:
- What might this student be protecting right now?
- What behavior is actually communication?
- Have I waited long enough to respond with clarity instead of assumption?

This practice often turns conflict into connection. It slows us down so we can lead relationally, not reactively.

Identity Agility Tools

Honor your evolution as much as your expertise.

You are not the same educator you were when you first entered this profession. That's not something you're meant to be. Identity agility is the ability to stay true to your core values while adapting and changing in real time. It's what enables you to lead with integrity—even when the system is inflexible or your own sense of self is shifting.

These tools support inner work like identity reflection, boundary-setting, and authentic presence. They're built to help you stay human in roles that often require emotional compartmentalization or self-erasure. You don't need to become a different person to succeed. You just need to be more of yourself—without apology.

7. Who Am I Here? Reflection Grid

Create a simple two-axis grid:
- Top row: My classroom | My staff room | My meetings
- Left column: "What parts of me show up?" | "What parts do I hide?"

Fill it out honestly. Then ask: What do I need to show up more whole across these spaces?

8. The Boundary Pause

Before saying yes to a request, consider:
- Does this align with who I am, or with who I think I have to be?
- What will it cost me emotionally to take this on?

Leadership without boundaries is not sustainable. This tool helps you say no with clarity, not guilt.

9. Identity Bridge Moments with Students

Choose a story from your own journey—one that reflects struggle, change, or becoming. Share it with vulnerability, not performance. Then ask your students:
- What's something you've had to unlearn or relearn lately?

These moments normalize growth. They build trust and model authenticity in real time.

10. The "Feel Your Way Through" Map

For when you can't think your way clear—but you can still feel your way forward.
Use this tool when you're moving through change, exhaustion, or quiet internal unrest. There are no rules—just reflections.

Journal your answers to the following:
- What am I grieving in my role right now, even if I haven't named it aloud?
- Where do I feel most disconnected—from my work, my students, or myself?
- What part of me is trying to speak louder lately? What have I been ignoring?
- What does my body know before my mind is ready to admit it?
- What's one truth I'm afraid to say, even just to myself?
- What would it feel like to lead from that truth, even just for one day?

This tool is not about solving. It's about softening. So you can start again with presence—not performance.

Final Words on Use

These tools are not meant to be comprehensive. They are intended to be human.
You might not use any of them formally. You might adapt one to better fit your students. That's the point. This isn't a script—it's a starting point.

As you keep reading, leading, and showing up despite exhaustion and complexity, let these tools serve as reminders.

You don't have to be perfect to lead with strength. You don't have to give up yourself to be effective.

You don't have to wait for permission to make change.

This is your classroom. Your voice. Your mirror.

This is your moment to lead, regardless.

PART IV

The Deep Work of Healing and Leading

DR. KARISSA THOMAS

The Teacher Who Never Asked for Help

Every school has a teacher who keeps everything running. The one everyone depends on. The one who says "I'm fine" even when they're falling apart. Maybe that teacher is you.

This part of the book reveals what's rarely spoken aloud: the emotional burden of being "the strong one," the healer, the stabilizer, the always-available anchor. It covers the cost of carrying a system on your shoulders while trying not to fall apart under its weight.

By now, you've read about leadership in action—how to respond to students, handle fragile teams, and show up despite disillusionment. However, this section is different. This is where we look inward.

Here, we ask: What does it mean to lead when you've been harmed by the very system you serve?

Chapter 16 opens with a story many educators recognize well — about quiet suffering, isolation disguised as resilience, and the harmful myth that asking for help shows weakness. It's not only about burnout but also about emotional depletion. It highlights what occurs when leaders are so dedicated to appearing strong for others that they forget to be kind to themselves.

And then we go even deeper.

In the upcoming interludes, we delve into higher education—where faculty, adjuncts, and staff often face the same invisibility under different names: intellectual work without acknowledgment, a student-first culture lacking educator care, and survival behind polished syllabi. These voices are important, too.

Part IV is where leadership intersects with honesty. It's where we reclaim the parts of ourselves that have been ignored, suppressed, or sacrificed for professionalism. It's where the Mosaic Intelligence Method™—emotional integrity, cultural flexibility, and identity agility—is not just a framework but a lifeline.

These pages won't fix everything, but they will reveal what's true. Sometimes, that's where healing starts.

This is the quiet, powerful, essential work.

This is the part of the story where wholeness becomes a way to resist. This is where we lead—differently.

CHAPTER 16

The Culture of Collective Care

The Teacher Who Never Asked for Help

Everyone admired Ms. Greene. She was consistent, generous, and calm under pressure. When new teachers arrived, they turned to her for guidance. When leadership faced a challenge, she was the one to solve it. She checked in on others, noticing when someone was struggling, and stayed late to help clean up after school events.

"The work was never meant to be carried alone. Healing is a shared act."

So when she finally broke—quietly, then all at once—no one saw it coming.

It wasn't just a single incident; it was the result of years. Years of giving more than she had. Of never being asked, "How are you—really?" Of carrying everyone else's well-being while silently neglecting her own.

She had received praise for her strength. However, what she truly needed was support.

The Myth of the Strong One

Every school has someone like Ms. Greene—the dependable teacher, the patient assistant principal, the mentor who always makes space for others. These educators are often recognized for their resilience, generosity, and ability to handle the emotional demands of a school.

However, strength without support results in exploitation.

And care that isn't mutual turns into sacrifice.

We can't keep leading like this—individuals quietly managing collective trauma while pretending we're fine. We don't need more lone heroes; we need systems of shared care. Because the upcoming work is too much for one person to handle alone.

What Collective Care Really Means

Collective care goes beyond just having a "wellness Wednesday." It isn't simply a self-care gift basket or a yoga class after school. While those activities can be helpful, they are not the core.

Collective care involves creating cultures where no one has to choose between their humanity and their professionalism. In such cultures, checking on each other isn't just for show—it's built into the system. Trust becomes a standard, not something earned. And boundaries are respected as an act of leadership, not as rebellion.

It means we don't allow the same people to carry the culture every year.

It means we address overwork as soon as we notice it—not just when it causes harm.

It means we stop seeing burnout as a personal failure and start recognizing it as a communal imbalance.

Courage Is a Team Sport

You've read throughout this book about courageous leadership. However, bravery cannot be maintained in isolation. Even the most daring educator will stumble without support.

To create courageous classrooms, we need courageous teams—people who hold each other accountable without shame, challenge one another with care, grieve together when difficulties arise in the community, and celebrate each other without competition.

Courage grows in environments where vulnerability isn't punished.

Leadership succeeds in teams where no one has to be everything for everyone.

What the Research Says

In my doctoral research on educator identity and emotional labor in international school settings, this theme emerged repeatedly: teachers often felt fragmented—forced to separate their inner lives from their professional roles to meet the relentless expectations of unfamiliar systems. One respondent shared, "I carry everyone's emotions, but I don't know where to put my own."

This isn't just emotional fatigue—it's a loss of identity.

A 2023 report from the Aspen Institute on educator well-being confirmed that collective efficacy—teams believing in and investing in each other—was one of the strongest predictors of sustained teacher motivation and student success, even in high-poverty schools.

The study highlighted that the most resilient teams not only shared common goals but also had relational safety, cultural humility, and routines of care woven into their weekly schedule. When collective care became a team norm, turnover declined, and trust strengthened—even under significant external pressures.

Building the Culture You Need

You don't need to wait for someone else to create this. You can model it—one conversation at a time, one boundary at a time, one moment of transparency that allows someone to exhale.

Ask your colleagues genuine questions—and stay long enough to hear the real answer.

Stop praising people for how much they tolerate.

Refuse to normalize dysfunction just because the school year requires it.

Asking for support isn't weakness; it's wisdom. When you show that wisdom, others will see they can be human too.

 MOSAIC IN ACTION

A brief exchange in a teacher lounge between two colleagues:

"You've seemed a little off this week. Want to take a walk instead of sitting through lunch duty?"

"I didn't even realize you noticed. Thank you—I think I needed that more than I knew."

Her Mosaic Intelligence in action:

Emotional Integrity: She recognized emotional shifts and responded genuinely, not performatively.

Cultural Flexibility: She provided care in a way that respected the other person's autonomy, not obligation.

Identity Agility: She rejected the idea of "just powering through" and permitted herself to accept support.

Opportunity: Culture starts when one person dares to check in—and stays present for the answer.

Enhancing Culture Through Collective Care

A strong school culture isn't created by moments of inspiration. It develops through the steady, everyday choices people make about how they support each other.

The research is clear: collective efficacy—the shared belief that we can succeed together—is more than just a feel-good idea. It's a key factor in resilience, retention, and results. But, collective efficacy cannot exist without collective care.

To build culture that lasts, we need to go beyond surface-level teamwork and create spaces for real connection. That involves setting aside time to check in—not just about progress reports or lesson plans, but about how people are truly doing.

It means resisting the urge to rush past someone's hesitation.

It means valuing well-being as much as performance.

It means unlearning the narratives that connect strength to suffering.

We need to stop applauding educators for how much they can endure and begin celebrating them for how well they care—for others, yes, but also for themselves.

Boundaries are not barriers to commitment; they are evidence of sustainability.

And every time an educator chooses rest over resentment, truth over performance, or presence over pretense, they reinforce a different kind of excellence—one rooted in wholeness, not depletion.

This cultural shift starts with individuals but spreads through modeling. You don't need a title to lead it. Every time you speak honestly about your limits, you create space for someone else to do the same. Every time you respond with empathy instead of critique, you strengthen trust.

Every time you ask a colleague how they're really doing—and genuinely mean it—you help create an environment where people don't just get through the school year; they grow from it.

This is what the Mosaic Intelligence Method™ looks like in practice—not just as theory, but as a real ethic of care. When emotional integrity guides how we lead, cultural flexibility shapes how we support, and identity agility influences how we respond, we move from transaction to transformation. We become systems of care—not just individuals within them.

In high-pressure environments, care can seem like a luxury. But when it's the standard, it changes the atmosphere.

People start to exhale. Walls fall down. Collaboration grows deeper. What was once a burden becomes a shared responsibility—

eased by trust, grounded in compassion, and carried by a team that remembers they are in this together.

Culture does not appear out of nowhere. It is created. Every time you choose care, you are laying the groundwork for something much stronger than just rules. You are building a community where everyone has the chance to thrive.

This Is Not Retaliation—It's Restoration

Let's be clear: this movement toward collective care is not about retaliation. It is not about rebellion, resistance for resistance's sake, or abandoning standards of excellence. It is about restoration.

Restoring dignity. Restoring balance. Restoring the humanity that has long been overshadowed by unrealistic demands and unspoken emotional labor.

Some may see the call for rest, boundaries, and emotional honesty as a threat to tradition or productivity. But in truth, it is an invitation—a call to rethink what sustainability and excellence mean in modern schools.

For this cultural shift to happen beyond the classroom, the entire system must respond.

Schools need to stop treating emotional well-being as solely an individual responsibility and start integrating it into how we operate.

This means school boards have a chance—and a duty—to lead differently.

- To revisit obsolete metrics of teacher effectiveness and student engagement
- To revise policies that encourage overextension rather than sustainability
- To fund and prioritize training that emphasizes care, cultural responsiveness, and emotional intelligence.
- To formalize practices that adapt to the changing realities of the educational ecosystem

Yes, this shift begins with people. But it cannot continue without policy.

Until those policies are in place, your engagement still counts. Your example still makes a difference.

You still have the power to influence not only your students' lives but also those of your colleagues. Your voice, boundaries, care, and honesty are significant—they are cultural seeds.

Because when we care for one another consistently and courageously, we do more than just survive a broken system.

We begin to remake it.

Lead Anyway Reflection

- Where in your leadership or team culture are you taking on more than your fair share—and has that effort been acknowledged?
- What unspoken expectations are you maintaining that could harm you or others?
- How can you tell when someone on your team is beginning to fracture—and what can you do besides just watch?
- What would collective care look like in your school if it were practiced every day instead of as a seasonal campaign?
- Who do you regularly check on—and who might need to check on you?

TOOL TO TRY:
Protect Sacred Time

Choose one weekly moment—early morning, after dismissal, during planning—and mark it as non-negotiable quiet. No meetings. No multitasking. Just stillness. Your clarity exists there.

TOOL TO TRY:
Ask the Clarity Question

When unsure about your next move, ask: "If I removed fear from this decision, what would I choose?" Sometimes, clarity is hidden beneath permission we haven't yet granted ourselves.

CHAPTER 17

When Leadership Fractures: Reclaiming the Pieces

Wholeness Is Not a Performance—It's a Return

There are moments in a leader's life when something breaks apart.
You're standing in front of a classroom, nodding during a meeting, coaching a colleague through a crisis—and yet, part of you feels like an observer. You're there, but not fully present. Your voice is heard, but your spirit feels distant. You've become someone the system will accept, but not entirely who you are.

This is the experience of leadership fragmentation. It's the internal divide that happens when educators have to choose between survival and authenticity, between emotional safety and institutional compliance. And it's more common than most people are willing to admit.

"You are allowed to reclaim your pieces. Broken isn't your identity— rebuilding is."

Fragmentation Is Not Failure

Fragmentation doesn't imply weakness or inauthenticity; it signifies adaptation.

You've learned how to show up in ways that minimize harm. You've learned how to speak with careful precision. You've learned how to control your facial expressions, voice, and presence to keep your job, maintain peace, or avoid retaliation.

But over time, that fragmentation has a cost: emotional dissonance, internal conflict, and a growing sense that something essential is being lost.

You begin to wonder:

Is this still who I am? How did I become this version of myself? What part of me have I sacrificed in the name of leadership?

The Body Remembers What the System Ignores

In my dissertation research, I examined how educators—particularly those dealing with the layered complexities of race, culture, gender, or migration—often internalize the very systems that marginalize them. This isn't just about professional burnout. It's about losing their sense of identity.

The body remembers everything, even when performance seems flawless. That heaviness in your chest, the numbness after yet another staff meeting, the quiet exhaustion that stays on weekends—these are not signs of weakness. They are signs of fragmentation.

I realized that teachers start to disconnect from their own voice, values, and vitality—not suddenly, but through repeated acts of emotional survival: one silenced truth, one over-commitment, one swallowed reaction at a time.

The more we adapt to fit a system that rarely truly sees us, the more we risk losing ourselves. Not because of failure, but out of instinct. Because part of us knows survival must come first.

But what has been divided can also be restored. Reclaiming it starts with recognizing the toll of fragmentation—not just in our work, but in our bodies, our identities, and our ability to show up whole.

Reclaiming Yourself Isn't Rebellion—It's Repair

Reclaiming the parts of yourself you've hidden or minimized isn't selfish. It's sacred.
It looks like:

- Allow your voice to return to its natural cadence, not its altered version.
- Lead with your story — not the polished version that fits the district newsletter.
- Fully experiencing your emotions without apologizing for how deep they are.
- Trust that your cultural lens, lived experience, accent, tone, softness, and age—everything about you—are part of your strength.

Repair isn't about returning to who you were before the fracture. It's about embracing who you are now—with more honesty, clarity, and compassion for the parts of yourself that had to go quiet to survive.
It's not about going back to innocence; it's about going back to wholeness.

The Mosaic Intelligence Method™ in Fractured Spaces

This is where the Mosaic Intelligence Method™ transcends a simple framework.
It becomes medicine.

Emotional Integrity means acknowledging when you're not fine instead of pretending. It involves trusting your intuition rather than diminishing it to please others. You lead from your true self, not just your job title.

Cultural Flexibility means you no longer code-switch to the point of erasure. You navigate different environments skillfully, but without abandoning your voice, your roots, or your rhythm.

Identity Agility means recognizing that your leadership can develop. You are permitted to outgrow the version of yourself the system has shaped—and fully step into the one your purpose now demands.

You don't have to lead as the fractured version the job conditioned you to become.

You get to lead as the whole version—the one that remembers who you are.

Fragmentation Can Be a Threshold

The cracks in our leadership are not signs of failure—they are openings. Invitations to reconnect with ourselves. Too often, we've been asked to split our identities, to lead from fractured parts, to perform a version of professionalism that erases the very pieces that make us whole. But we were never meant to lead through self-erasure.

We were never meant to prove our worth by abandoning our truth. The fractured places—moments of rupture, silence, and internal conflict—can become our strongest. Because it is in those spaces that our clarity returns, our voice deepens, and our leadership begins to heal. This is the core of leadership: not shaping yourself into what others will accept, but reclaiming who you are. Only from that place can true change begin.

 MOSAIC IN ACTION

Dr. Amira, a department chair at a large urban college, realized she had stopped using her native dialect when greeting students—something she once did with pride. After years of being told her tone was "too sharp" or "too direct," she had softened her voice until it was almost unrecognizable to herself. One day, a student whispered, "I miss your voice." That moment opened something up. She started gradually bringing her full voice back into meetings, lectures, and emails. Not to prove a point—but to return to herself.

Her Mosaic Intelligence in action:

Emotional Integrity: She acknowledged the grief of what she had silenced.

Cultural Flexibility: She confidently embraced her multilingual identity.

Identity Agility: She released the version of herself molded by constant approval—and started leading with authenticity.

Opportunity: Sometimes the strongest leadership move is to speak in your own voice again.

Lead Anyway Reflection

- Which parts of yourself have you had to break apart to succeed in your role?
- How has your leadership changed to meet institutional expectations that don't align with your truth?
- Where in your body or spirit do you feel the impact of fragmentation?
- What would wholeness look like in your leadership today—not five years from now?
- Who or what allows you to return to your true self?

> **TOOL TO TRY:**
> **Make the Micro-Moment Count**

In passing moments—between bells, in the cafeteria, at dismissal—pause to say: "I see you." A brief check-in can change the trajectory of a student's day.

> **TOOL TO TRY:**
> **Practice the Hallway Phrase**

Have a go-to phrase ready for hallway leadership: "I've got five seconds, but I'm here." "Let's circle back—I want to hear more." Even short words can have a lasting impact.

CHAPTER 18

Lead Anyway—Now and Next

Sustaining Wholeness in Systems That Still Forget You

You've come this far. Through the fog, the fractures, the quiet breakthroughs, and the silent breakdowns. You've asked the tough questions. You've viewed your leadership not just as a role but as a reflection of your truth. You've reclaimed the pieces you once thought had to be lost to survive.

But now what?

This chapter isn't about looking backward. It's about moving forward—toward a way of leading that is sustainable, spacious, and sacred.

"Sustainability isn't just a strategy. It's how we protect the soul of this work."

Systems May Not Change Overnight—But You Can Lead Differently Tomorrow

You aren't waiting for the institution to catch up. You're leading with clarity all along. You're not putting your wholeness on hold until next semester, the next principal, or the next policy cycle. You're practicing it now.

You're not demanding perfection from yourself—you're committed to alignment.

That is what leadership looks like.

Sustainable leadership doesn't mean you never feel drained. It means you have practices that restore you. It means you stop seeking validation from systems that lost your worth long ago. It means you direct your energy where real change can happen—in your students, your presence, your voice, your alignment.

You're not here to manipulate appearances. You're here to demonstrate what wholeness looks like in real time.

The Quiet Power of Consistent Presence

Some of the most courageous leadership isn't showy. It's the quiet choice to speak up in a meeting when you're the only one.

It's the refusal to sacrifice your boundaries to play the role of a "team player."

It's the decision to honor a student's humanity when policy would rather you punish.

Your presence breaks patterns. The way you behave within the system sends messages, even when no one notices. You're not just teaching content. You're showing what it means to live and lead with integrity.

That impact doesn't fit on a spreadsheet.

But it goes somewhere more important: into culture. Into legacy. Into how others will lead after you.

Leadership Is a Daily Practice—Not a Destination

We don't achieve emotional integrity once and for all.

We keep returning to it.

We don't fully master cultural flexibility in theory.

We live it through tension.

We don't claim to resolve identity issues quickly and walk away completely healed.

We wrestle, reframe, and come back again.

Your leadership isn't a fixed state; it's a fluid practice. Each day you choose to lead with alignment, you redefine what leadership looks like.

The Mosaic Intelligence Method™ as a Legacy Lens

As you progress, let the Mosaic Intelligence Method™ serve as your perspective:

Emotional Integrity: Pause before reacting. Lead from what is true, not what is expected. Let your emotional presence be part of your professional strength.

Cultural Flexibility: Remain open while staying true to yourself. You can connect across differences without sacrificing your depth.

Identity Agility: Don't stay stuck in the version that first succeeded. Allow your leadership to evolve with your healing, joy, and purpose.

Let this be your framework—not for perfection, but for wholeness. Not for performance, but for presence.

MOSAIC IN ACTION

Tanya, an instructional coach in a large urban district, was once told she was "too passionate" about equity. She learned to tone herself down, focus on data points, and avoid confronting difficult topics. But over time, that silence wore on her. She started reintroducing parts of her voice—first in hallway conversations, then in coaching sessions, and eventually in district-wide trainings.

Her Mosaic Intelligence in action:

Emotional Integrity: She acknowledged the discomfort of remaining silent and chose to speak from honesty.

Cultural Flexibility: She adapted her language for different audiences—without diluting her message.

Identity Agility: She redefined what it meant to be "professional" on her own terms.

The result? Her work now influences district policy—not because she demanded it, but because her presence made it undeniable.

Lead Anyway Reflection

- What emotional patterns are you ready to release so you can lead from a place of wholeness?
- How can you shift from performance to presence in your leadership interactions this week?
- Where have you adopted systems that no longer help you—and how might you rewrite those scripts?
- Who are you becoming—not just in title, but in reality?
- What kind of legacy do you want your leadership to leave behind?

This isn't the end.
It's your comeback.
Keep leading. Keep returning. Keep becoming.
Lead anyway—because your wholeness is the most radical leadership tool you have.

TOOL TO TRY:
Affirm Your Inner Anchor

When everything external feels uncertain, pause and say: "I'm still here. I still care. That's enough to begin again." Repeat as needed.

TOOL TO TRY:
Return to the Why

Write your "why" on a sticky note or inside your planner. Read it before the hardest days. You don't have to feel inspired every day—but you can always lead from your deeper reason.

INTERLUDE

Leading While Healing: When You've Been Harmed by the System

There is a distinct kind of ache that occurs when you are asked to lead and heal within the same system that once erased you.
It's the ache of walking into rooms where decisions are made without you—yet still affect you.
It's the pain of being praised for your resilience while secretly bleeding inside.
It's the dissonance of being called "the voice of diversity" in meetings where no one truly listens when you speak.
And still—you lead.
You show up for students who resemble you, feel like you, or are walking paths you once fought to survive. You offer what you never received. You teach from scars that haven't fully healed. You lead with heart in spaces that haven't always honored your humanity.
That is more than brave. It is sacred.

The Cost of Being the First, the Only, or the One Who Speaks Up

Maybe you were the first Black woman in your department.
Maybe you're the only openly queer educator on your campus.
Maybe you've been labeled "too much" for asking the right questions—or "too quiet" for not engaging in the politics of the room.
Whatever your story, the cost of leading while healing is real.

You carry the burden of representation—the expectation to stay professional even when provoked, the pressure to teach, inspire, and challenge, all while protecting your peace.

It is exhausting. And no, you're not imagining it.

This is the emotional labor that systems rarely acknowledge but constantly require. It's the invisible cost of being the cultural translator, emotional anchor, uncredited policy editor, and moral conscience in institutional conversations that often resist real change.

As my dissertation findings revealed, educators in marginalized identity positions often experience "performative inclusion"—where diversity is publicly celebrated but privately unsupported. This creates a persistent undercurrent of cognitive dissonance: being expected to represent while never truly being seen.

You Are Not Broken—The System Is

If no one's told you lately, the tension you feel isn't a flaw in your leadership—it's a sign that you're awake. That your spirit hasn't hardened to the hypocrisy. That your humanity hasn't conformed to the machine.

You are not overly sensitive.
You are not overly complicated.
You are not overly emotional.
You are navigating systems not built for your full potential—and still choosing to lead.

That is a revolutionary act.

You Deserve Restoration, Too

You don't just deserve a seat at the table.

You deserve rest, repair, and spaces where your story doesn't need to be translated to be believed.

Healing while leading means:

- Identifying the cause of the pain without downplaying its impact.

- Seeking joy even in places that once silenced you.
- Setting boundaries that don't need explanation.
- Refusing to pour from a soul that is constantly scraped.

It means being honest about the toll—and still showing up based on truth, not performance.

It involves selecting wholeness in a system that frequently rewards fragmentation.

Lead Without Leaving Yourself Behind

You do not owe the system your silence.
You do not owe your students your trauma reenacted as overwork.
You do not have to be twice as good to be taken half as seriously.
What you owe—to yourself, your story, and the younger version of you still watching—is your wholeness.
You are permitted to lead while healing.
You are permitted to protect your happiness. You are permitted to choose gentleness over just surviving.
And when you do, you demonstrate what liberation looks like in real time.
This is what the **Mosaic Intelligence Method™** calls us toward:

Emotional Integrity involves acknowledging what you carry without shame.

Cultural Flexibility in navigating systems without sacrificing your values.

Identity Agility is about choosing who you become, not just surviving who you've been.

Leading while healing is not a sign of weakness. It is profoundly wise.
And it is how we break cycles of harm—by refusing to pass them on.

Lead Anyway Reflection

- What aspects of your leadership have been affected by harm, and are you still reenacting those patterns today?
- Where are you supposed to express your identity rather than just be accepted into it?
- What does healing mean for you — not just for your students?
- Who is safe enough for you to fall apart with—and how can you cultivate more of that?
- What version of leadership would honor both your scars and your strengths?

INTERLUDE

Lead Anyway in the Academy: Faculty, Adjuncts, and the Hidden Curriculum of Survival

The Silence Between the Semesters

Dr. Morgan read their student evaluations in silence. The comments were mixed. Some praised their brilliance. Others said they talked too much about race. One student noted, "This class made me uncomfortable—but I needed that." Another simply wrote, "She was intimidating." That line lingered—not because it was fair, but because it would be used. In tenure discussions. In hiring meetings. In conversations where identity was under review, whether acknowledged or not.

This is the unspoken curriculum of academia: demonstrate intellectual rigor, but never with too much passion. Encourage dialogue, but only if it doesn't harm the institution's reputation. Teach the future, but don't challenge the foundation too openly. Still, educators like Dr. Morgan lead regardless.

The Emotional Cost of Academic Performance

Higher education often promises intellectual freedom, but what it often delivers is more complicated: performative inclusion, isolation disguised as independence, and hyper-productivity seen as a measure of worth. Faculty are expected to publish, advise, mentor, innovate, respond, grade, and teach—all while managing identity politics, institutional inequality, and the instability of short-term contracts.

Adjuncts handle full course loads without benefits or a sense of belonging. Tenure-track faculty must navigate cultures that rarely allow them to express their true selves. Staff professionals work within policy limits but bear the emotional burden of student crises. This is not a failure of passion—it is a failure of structure. And yet, despite these challenges, many educators continue to build spaces of liberation. They model wholeness. They lead—not because the system recognizes them, but because their students deserve more.

The Intellectual-Emotional Divide

The academy values knowledge but not always wisdom. Theory is highly regarded, while identity, emotion, and lived experience are often seen as distractions. However, true teaching requires presence. It demands emotional fluency and authenticity that cannot be peer-reviewed but leaves a lasting impact.

Leadership in the academy appears in the professor who clearly recognizes historical erasure, in the advisor who stays late to support a first-generation student through academic or identity uncertainties, and in the department chair who says, "This policy doesn't reflect our humanity—we need to revise it." These actions rarely show up on a CV, but they are woven into students, cultures, and institutional memory.

What the Research Says

A 2023 study published in *The Journal of Higher Education* found that emotional labor among faculty—especially women, faculty of color, and LGBTQ+ professors—is both vital and often undervalued. These faculty members frequently received the highest ratings in student trust and engagement, yet their efforts were the least recognized or supported by the institution.

Another report by the American Council on Education showed that students who feel emotionally connected to even one faculty or staff member—especially during their first year—are much more likely to persist and graduate. That success isn't always linked to course content but to the presence of care and connection.

Wholeness in the Academy Isn't a Luxury

Leading in higher education involves choosing alignment over approval. It means mentoring without martyrdom and setting boundaries in a culture that often rewards overextension. It entails recognizing what you carry and refusing to bear it all alone.

As my dissertation research highlighted, many educators—especially those working within Western or international systems—experience identity fragmentation: the pressure to split their personal and professional selves to survive. They often have to hide emotional labor, act neutral, and detach parts of themselves to maintain credibility. However, divided leaders cannot create whole communities.

You are not responsible for saving the institution. However, you may be called to humanize it. Not by rejecting rigor, but by redefining it. Not by silencing scholarship, but by allowing your full story to inform it. Not by walking away in silence, but by continuing forward with clarity and presence—even when the system does not applaud.

The future of the academy isn't in its rankings; it's in its relationships. It exists in the classroom, the hallway conversation, and the email reply at just the right moment. The places where you choose to show up fully—that's where transformation begins.

This is what the Mosaic Intelligence Method™ looks like in academic settings. Emotional integrity enables you to lead confidently without shrinking back. Cultural flexibility prepares you to engage without erasing others. Identity agility allows you to incorporate all parts of yourself—intellectual, emotional, and embodied—without sacrifice. When we lead from wholeness, we move beyond just surviving the institution and start actively shaping it.

DR. KARISSA THOMAS

 MOSAIC IN ACTION

The Adjunct Who Rewrote the Culture Without a Title

At a mid-sized university in the Northeast, an adjunct instructor named Selina quietly became the emotional anchor of her department. Although she had no office and worked semester to semester, she made it a point to greet each student by name and learn something personal about them by the second week of class. When a student disclosed food insecurity, she connected them to support. When a new colleague expressed uncertainty about navigating DEI expectations, she shared her course materials without hesitation.

She wasn't on the diversity committee or invited to faculty summits. However, when the department faced backlash over a racially insensitive email, students and faculty turned to Selina. She organized a listening circle, modeled emotionally intelligent communication, and pushed for systemic accountability—even though it wasn't her "role." Her leadership wasn't about a title; it was about her presence.

Her Mosaic Intelligence in action:

Emotional Integrity: She responded to the community's pain without numbing her own exhaustion, exemplifying care without breaking down.

Cultural Flexibility: She connected with each student and colleague where they were, incorporating empathy into policy discussions and conflict resolution.

Identity Agility: Instead of shrinking her identity to conform to academia's standards, she leveraged it to expand the sense of belonging.

The opportunity:

You don't need institutional permission to lead based on your values. All you need is clarity, courage, and the willingness to embody your leadership—not just teach it.

Lead Anyway Reflection
For Higher Ed Leaders and Educators

- Which aspects of your identity have you been told to silence in order to be "respected" in academic spaces?
- In which areas have you excelled emotionally, intellectually, or professionally without receiving recognition?
- What version of academia are you presenting to your students—and is it the one you genuinely believe in?
- How do you stay true to your humanity while following institutional expectations?
- What would leading in your department, classroom, or field mean for you?

CLOSING REFLECTIONS

LEGACY LETTER TO EDUCATORS

A Closing Word from Dr. Karissa Thomas

Dear Educator,

If no one has mentioned this to you recently: thank you.
Not just for teaching—but for caring.
For carrying what the system rarely sees.
For staying when it would have been easier to walk away.
For believing in students who had not yet found their voice.
For leading even when you felt invisible.

You may never fully realize the impact you've had. But somewhere, a student stands a little taller because of you. Somewhere, a colleague breathes a little easier because of your calm. Somewhere, a classroom feels just a bit safer because of your presence.

This book was never about perfection. It was about honesty. It emphasized a form of leadership that allows space for doubt, fatigue, joy, and courage. It was about reclaiming the parts of yourself that the system taught you to suppress—and choosing to lead from your whole self anyway.

The truth is: systems may change slowly, but people influence each other immediately.

And you?

You are quietly changing lives every day, in a lasting way.

Remember that your wholeness is connected to your leadership; it is an essential part of it.

You don't have to disappear to make a difference. You don't have to overextend yourself to prove your worth. You don't have to suffer to be seen.

Lead with your truth.
Lead through your alignment.
Lead from your restoration.

Because your legacy isn't measured by the number of lessons you deliver or the hours you log.

Your legacy is the emotional blueprint you leave behind.

And that legacy—it lives in how people feel when they are around you.

It lives in who they become because of your belief in them.

Lead with courage.
Lead with care.
Lead as if your presence matters — because it does.
And when the system forgets who you are, remember this:
You still have the power to lead, anyway.

With respect and solidarity,

Dr. Karissa Thomas

LEAD ANYWAY: FINAL REFLECTIONS AND COURAGE QUESTIONS

A Companion Section with Journal Prompts, Scenarios, and Leadership Micro-Practices

You Made It Here on Purpose

Finishing this book doesn't mean the fog has fully cleared. It means you are learning to lead through it—with greater clarity, more courage, and a rising sense of self-trust. You're no longer waiting to be rescued by the system. You're reshaping it from within, through your presence, your choices, and your refusal to lead in fragments.

This companion section is designed to give you space to pause, explore more deeply, and return to your leadership with renewed purpose. The reflections, micro-practices, and real-world leadership scenarios are meant to gently stretch you, not to overwhelm. You don't need to complete them all at once, nor do you have to get everything "right." Just stay honest. Your growth isn't about how much you do but about how fully you show up.

Journal Prompts for the Brave Educator

Use the questions below as starting points for reflection, journaling, or discussion with trusted colleagues.

- What part of this book resonated with you the most, and why?
- Where are you still leading from a place of survival, and what would it take to move toward wholeness?
- What story are you telling about what leadership "should" look like—and is it still true?
- How do you want students, colleagues, or your team to feel in your presence—and what needs to change for that to happen more often?
- What does it really mean to lead when no one is watching?

Real-World Leadership Scenarios

These brief leadership dilemmas encourage reflection on how you handle pressure, ambiguity, and power dynamics in your everyday environment.

Scenario 1: A coworker shares frustration during a staff meeting. You agree with their point, but you're worried speaking out may make you seem "difficult." → What does it look like to speak up regardless—and to do so with both confidence and compassion?

Scenario 2: A student challenges your authority in a way that triggers something deeper in you—old wounds, identity tension, or fear of being disrespected.
→ What part of you needs tending before you can respond with presence instead of reaction?

Scenario 3: Your school adopts a new initiative that doesn't reflect your community's genuine needs. You're not in a position of formal power.
→ What quiet forms of resistance—or creative leadership—can you practice anyway?

Micro-Practices for the Week Ahead

Try one or more of these gentle leadership actions in the coming days. Each one aims to reconnect you with your values and demonstrate a more humane way of leading.

- Start your day with mindfulness, not just tasks. Before opening your email, spend two minutes grounding yourself. Ask: Who do I want to be today, beyond what I need to do?
- Ask one brave question in a meeting. Not to challenge authority, but to show critical curiosity. Focus on depth rather than agreement.
- Write a brief acknowledgment note to a student, colleague, or yourself. Recognizing emotions is a form of leadership.
- End one day this week without feeling guilty. Leave on time. Say no when necessary. Protect your humanity with the same energy you use to care for your students.

This Isn't the End—It's Your Re-entry

Leadership isn't just a title. It's a practice—a daily choice to stay human in a system that takes parts of you. As you finish these pages, remember what matters most: clarity, compassion, and the quiet confidence that you were never meant to lead in pieces. You were meant to lead whole.
Continue choosing wholeness.
Continue choosing courage.
Continue choosing to lead—anyway.

Suggested Ways to Use the Book

1. **Monthly Staff Book Club** — Select one chapter each month and use the "Lead Anyway Reflection" prompts to facilitate discussion.

2. **Leadership Team Retreat** — Use specific chapters (such as Chapters 1, 5, 10, 14, and 16) as foundational texts to reset school vision and relational leadership practices.
3. **New Teacher Orientation** — Include essential chapters in onboarding to establish a tone of compassionate, sustainable leadership from the beginning.
4. **Department-Based Dialogues** — Enable safe-space sessions within content teams by utilizing chapter-aligned journal questions.
5. **PD Day Series** — Spread six chapters across three professional development days and link each to a live leadership activity.
6. **Wellness & Retention Strategy** — Refer to Chapters 3, 5, and 16 to help teams identify burnout patterns and model collective care.
7. **Equity & Inclusion Council Tool** — Use the Interlude, Higher Ed Interlude, and Chapters 11 and 12 to foster identity discussions and challenge unfair norms.

Where to Begin, Based on Role

- **Assistant Principals** → Should begin with Chapters 6, 10, and 14. These chapters cover leading from the middle, holding emotional space, and modeling wellness without sacrificing authority.
- **Principals & Coaches** → Start with Chapters 1, 7, and 15. These offer clarity on modern instructional leadership, wholeness as a strategy, and reshaping school culture.
- **Teachers** → Start with Chapters 2, 3, 4, and 12. These cover presence in the classroom, resilience, identity, and student voice.
- **Adjunct Faculty or Professors** → Read the Higher Ed Interlude and Chapters 9 and 13 for insights into navigating institutions and maintaining emotional presence in the academy.

Interested in Going Deeper?

School and district licenses for *Lead Anyway* are available, along with facilitation guides, team discussion templates, and PD slide decks.

Coming Soon: A certification pathway for *Mosaic Intelligence Method*™ facilitators—designed for leaders ready to implement emotionally intelligent, culturally responsive, and identity-anchored leadership in their schools and organizations.

If you or your team are ready to deepen this work through coaching, cohort facilitation, or school-wide alignment, contact us directly using the information provided in this book.

You're not just reading a book. You're creating a better culture—one decision, one conversation, one act of courage at a time.

Bringing This Book to Your School

A Practical Invitation to Lead Anyway—Together

This book was written for you, but it was never meant to stay just with you.

What would change if your whole team read this book together—one chapter at a time, one conversation at a time, one act of courage at a time?

What if teachers didn't have to lead alone? If assistant principals didn't have to bear the tension by themselves? If every meeting, every PD day, and every staff conversation became a chance for emotional clarity, shared vision, and cultural healing?

You don't need to overhaul everything to lead differently.
You just need to get started.

For Teams and School Leaders

If you're a principal, coach, department chair, or district leader looking to:

- Foster a culture of emotional trust among your staff.
- Enhance retention with relational leadership
- Reignite clarity, engagement, and purpose among exhausted educators
- Provide genuine professional development that meets actual educator needs.

Then *Lead Anyway* can serve as the foundation of that work.
This book was created not only for reflection but also for transformation when used within a community.

Professional Learning Options

Customized packages are available for:

- **Staff Book Studies** (with facilitator guides + discussion prompts)
- **Leadership Retreats** (for APs, teacher leaders, and central office teams)
- **PD Workshops** (1-hour sessions or full-day trainings, virtual or in-person)
- **Keynote Sessions** (conference and convocation speaking engagements)
- **Train-the-Trainer Licensing** (for organizations ready to embed this culture systemically)

All trainings are grounded in the **Mosaic Intelligence Method™**, a leadership framework that develops:

- **Emotional Integrity**
- **Cultural Flexibility**
- **Identity Agility**

These are the new non-negotiables of sustainable leadership in education.

Let's Partner

To learn more or bring *Lead Anyway* to your school, campus, or district:

Website: drkarissathomas.net

You are not meant to carry this alone.
Let's build together.
Let's lead anyway—together.

APPENDICES

REFERENCES

Aspen Institute. (2023). *The well-being of educators: Building collective care in schools.* Aspen Education & Society Program.

Brackett, M. (2019). *Permission to feel: Unlocking the power of emotions to help our kids, ourselves, and our society thrive.* Celadon Books.

Carnegie Foundation for the Advancement of Teaching. (2022). *Educator well-being and instructional effectiveness: A national review of school leadership strategies.*

CASEL. (2021). *The impact of SEL on educator well-being and student outcomes.* Collaborative for Academic, Social, and Emotional Learning.

Learning Policy Institute. (2022). *The elements of a positive school climate: Supporting student and teacher well-being.* https://learningpolicyinstitute.org

RAND Corporation. (2022). *Teacher well-being and stress during the COVID-19 pandemic.* RAND Education and Labor.

Search Institute. (2021). *Developmental relationships and student outcomes: A longitudinal study of student-adult connections in school.* Search Institute.

Stanford Center for Opportunity Policy in Education. (2023). *Student voice and equity-centered schools: Engagement strategies and outcomes.* Stanford University.

Wallace Foundation. (2021). *How principals affect students and schools: A systematic synthesis of two decades of research.* Wallace Foundation.

GLOSSARY

Adjunct Faculty — Part-time instructors in higher education, often hired on a contractual basis without long-term job security or benefits.

Belonging — The feeling of being seen, accepted, and valued for one's full identity within a group, institution, or community. Belonging is crucial to well-being and engagement, especially in diverse learning environments.

Burnout — A state of ongoing physical and emotional exhaustion, often resulting from extended stress or overwork, especially in caregiving or educational professions.

Care-Centered Leadership — An approach to leadership that emphasizes emotional presence, trust, and human sustainability rather than just compliance, control, or efficiency.

Collective Care — A shared approach to well-being where emotional support, boundaries, and trust are integrated into workplace culture and team interactions.

Cultural Flexibility — The ability to adapt, relate, and respond respectfully across diverse cultural and identity contexts while staying true to oneself.

Emotional Integrity — Leading with honesty and awareness of your own emotions, while creating a safe space for others to do the same without shame or suppression.

Emotional Labor — The often unseen work of managing your own emotions and the emotional responses of others to meet expectations, keep harmony, or prevent conflict. It's especially common in caregiving and teaching roles.

Identity Agility — The ability to navigate, adapt, and remain true to one's identity while operating in diverse, ever-changing environments.

Instructional Wholeness — Teaching from an integrated sense of self instead of from fragmented roles or expectations; respecting personal boundaries, emotions, and values in the classroom.

Leadership from the Middle — The practice of influencing change and demonstrating emotionally intelligent leadership without necessarily holding top administrative positions. Often applies to assistant principals, coaches, or teacher-leaders.

Microboundaries — Small, intentional choices that protect your emotional bandwidth and conserve energy—such as pausing before responding, setting time limits, or choosing when to engage. These cumulative actions foster sustainability.

Mosaic Intelligence Method™ — A leadership framework developed by Dr. Karissa Thomas that combines emotional integrity, cultural adaptability, and identity agility. It helps leaders and educators handle pressure, honor their full identities, and create inclusive, care-focused environments.

Professional Fragmentation — The internal split that happens when educators feel pressured to suppress or compartmentalize parts of their identity to meet institutional expectations. Over time, this can undermine authenticity and well-being.

Psychological Safety — a workplace or group environment where people feel comfortable speaking up, taking risks, and being vulnerable without fear of punishment or humiliation.

Relational Leadership — A leadership approach that emphasizes trust, empathy, and connection rather than hierarchy, authority, or control.

Restorative Practice — An approach to discipline and community-building that focuses on accountability, repairing relationships, and inclusive dialogue instead of punishment.

Student Voice — The inclusion and amplification of student perspectives, experiences, and ideas in the learning process and school decision-making.

Systemic Fatigue — The emotional exhaustion that comes from dealing with unfair, bureaucratic, or dehumanizing systems over time, especially for educators from historically marginalized groups.

Teacher Agency — The ability of educators to act independently, make informed choices, and influence the conditions of their professional environment.

Wholeness — A state of personal and professional harmony where all parts of the self—emotional, intellectual, cultural, and spiritual—are respected and integrated into daily leadership and teaching.

ABOUT THE AUTHOR

Dr. Karissa Thomas is an award-winning author, global leadership strategist, and creator of the Mosaic Intelligence Method™. With over ten years of experience in both classrooms and cross-cultural leadership environments, she helps leaders respond to pressure with emotional integrity, cultural fluency, and lasting clarity.

Dr. Thomas holds a doctorate in Educational Leadership and an Executive MBA. Her work connects research with real-world practice, helping educators, executive teams, and policy leaders create systems based on human dignity, relational trust, and inclusive change.

She is the author of several leadership books, including *Leading After the Storm*, *The Mosaic Way Field Glossary*, and *Claim the Lead*. She is also the founder of multiple professional platforms focused on resilient leadership and emotional intelligence.

To find out more about her leadership training, licensing opportunities, or speaking engagements, visit drkarissathomas.net

Licensing, Facilitation, and Certification

If you're ready to bring *Lead Anyway* to your school, district, or organization, or to be certified in the Mosaic Intelligence Method™:

- School and district-wide licensing
- Professional development facilitation guides
- Certification pathways for Mosaic Intelligence facilitators
- Custom coaching and keynote offerings

Connect & Share

We'd love to hear how this book is shaping your leadership.

Share your insights and tag us on social media:
Instagram: @mosaicintelligencemethod
LinkedIn: Dr. Karissa Thomas
mosaicintelligencemethod.com
Use the hashtag **#LeadAnywayBook** to join the conversation.

Continue the Journey

If this book resonated with you, consider:

- Starting a campus-wide book circle using the Final Reflection tools
- Inviting Dr. Karissa Thomas to speak at your next PD or retreat
- Becoming a licensed facilitator of the Mosaic Intelligence Method™

The work doesn't end here. But neither does your courage.
You are ready.
You are needed.
Lead anyway.

Lead Anyway

Teaching Through the Fog When the System Stops Seeing You
By Dr. Karissa Thomas

Leadership has evolved. Have you?

In an era when schools ask more but see educators less, *Lead Anyway* presents a new blueprint for leadership—focused not on perfection or policy, but on presence, wholeness, and emotional integrity.

This isn't a book about systems. It's a book about the people inside them—teachers, assistant principals, adjuncts, and faculty who are quietly transforming culture through courage, care, and clarity.

Drawing from real stories, global leadership experience, and more than ten years in education, Dr. Karissa Thomas introduces the **Mosaic Intelligence Method™**—a transformative framework built on three core pillars:

Emotional Integrity
Cultural Flexibility
Identity Agility

Whether you're burned out, breaking new ground, or somewhere in between, this book will meet you where you are—and remind you that leadership doesn't start when things get easier. It starts the moment you decide to lead anyway.

Includes:

- Reflective prompts & real-life scenarios
- Micro-practices for courageous leadership
- Practical tools for collective care & team healing
- PD guides and certification opportunities for school-wide use

DR. KARISSA THOMAS

Dr. Karissa Thomas is a global leadership strategist, educator, and creator of the Mosaic Intelligence Method™. She has trained leaders across the U.S., the Middle East, and beyond, helping them lead with courage, clarity, and care.